# The Book On Operational Excellence

## From High-Level Strategy to Ground-Level Execution

**The Book On Series**

**Julian Mercer**

Published by The Book On Publishing, 2025.

First edition. July 30, 2025.

Website: https://thebookon.ca

Substack: https://thebookonpublishing.substack.com/

The Book On Operational Excellence: From High-Level Strategy to Ground-Level Execution

**First edition. July 30, 2025.**

Copyright © 2025 The Book On Publishing
ISBN: 978-1-997795-77-3

Written by Julian Mercer

# The Book On Series

# Read This First

This is not a book designed to entertain you. It's not here to charm, to soothe, or to hold your hand. It won't dazzle you with stories, metaphors, or motivational fluff. What you're having is a tool, an instruction manual written for people who are serious about learning, executing, and thinking at a higher level.

Every book in The Book On Series is built on a single premise: clarity beats complexity. We believe that when you strip away the noise, the emotions, the marketing spin, and the cultural rituals of "self-help," what's left is raw, unembellished instruction. That's what these books offer.

They are dry by design. Not because we don't care about language or narrative, but because when you're building something that matters, you don't need more distractions. You need a clear architecture. Mental scaffolding. Direction that respects your intelligence.

Each title in this series takes on a specific domain: decision-making, clarity, strategy, leverage, uncertainty, and drills deep. Not in sweeping generalizations, but in applied frameworks. These are books for builders, operators, founders, tacticians, and thinkers—people who don't just consume knowledge but operationalize it.

You'll find no chapter-long anecdotes here. No self-congratulatory memoirs. No bullet-point platitudes. Instead, what you'll get is structured insight: argument, example, application. The tone is direct. The prose is sober. The ideas are designed to be lifted out and used.

You won't be coddled, but you won't be misled either.

There's a place in the world for lyrical, emotional, story-driven books, and this isn't that place. This is a workspace. A blueprint. A conversation for people who are ready to act, not just absorb.

We respect your time and your intellect.

Welcome to The Book On Series.

# Table of Contents

# Preface

## Why This Book, and Why Now

In fast-moving organizations, strategy is often the hero. Vision, ambition, and innovation dominate the conversation. But ask any operator what holds teams back, and the answer rarely starts with strategy. It begins with execution: work that's slow, unclear, redundant, or misaligned. Not because the people are wrong, but because the system isn't right.

This book was written for leaders who feel that tension. Who knows, they've outgrown improvisation but aren't sure how to scale discipline without killing creativity. It's for COOs, GMs, team leads, and anyone responsible for making work not just move, but move well.

The concepts here were built in the field, tested in high-growth startups, nonprofits, services orgs, and complex regulated industries. They're not drawn from a single methodology or school of thought. Instead, they reflect a set of design principles: clarity over chaos, feedback over guesswork, and integrity over performance theater.

If you've ever felt the weight of a system that makes good work harder than it needs to be, this book is for you. Not to inspire. But to equip.

# Introduction

## The Operational Excellence Imperative

Operational excellence isn't just a management ideal; it's the difference between resilience and rot. In any system, the absence of clarity compounds silently until it explodes publicly: in failed launches, missed targets, exhausted teams, and reputations that decay from within. The organizations that thrive aren't the ones with the best ideas; they're the ones that can execute cleanly under pressure, at scale, and without burning out their people. In that sense, operational excellence is not a bonus. It's the scaffolding that holds everything else up.

There's a moment in every leader's journey when they realize that vision, talent, and ambition aren't enough. It doesn't happen during the launch or the early wins. It happens later, often quietly, when the cracks begin to show, not in the product, not even in the strategy, but in the system itself. Deadlines start slipping. Coordination falters—accountability blurs. And the same fire that once fueled momentum begins to burn through the floorboards. At first, it feels like bad luck. A tough quarter. A people problem. A temporary stretch of chaos. But eventually, if you're honest, the truth becomes unavoidable. The chaos isn't temporary. It's structural. It's baked into how you operate. And if it's not confronted, it will consume you.

This book is written for that moment. It's not for the idealist dreaming of a perfect strategy. It's not for the cheerleader who thinks culture alone can fix execution. And it's certainly not for the founder who believes growth excuses dysfunction. This book is for the builder who's ready to do something more complex and more courageous: to choose discipline over improvisation, to build systems instead of patching symptoms, and to operationalize excellence not as a slogan but as a daily standard. Because operational excellence is not a one-time project or a phase to power through, it's not what you do after the product works or once the market is won. It's the thing that determines whether your product stays relevant, your team stays healthy, and your vision becomes durable.

The lie that kills most companies isn't that they didn't care about excellence. It's that they believed they could afford to wait. They thought operational clarity was something to clean up later. They believed high-functioning systems would naturally emerge from a strong team and good intentions. But that's not how it works. Execution entropy is the default. Without intentional design, your organization will drift. Roles will blur. Systems will clog. Decisions will bottleneck. And eventually, the complexity will outweigh the competence.

You've seen it. The startup that launches quickly but ultimately unravels under its weight. The enterprise that runs on reputation while drowning in process. The NGO has noble goals, but lacks the infrastructure to deliver them effectively. These stories aren't rare. They're common. And they're not about intelligence or ethics or effort. They're about operations. Or more precisely, the lack of operational rigor when it mattered most.

The organizations that endure don't do so by luck. They do so by building a kind of invisible muscle, a backbone of reliable systems, clean decisions, crisp execution, and continuous learning. They make fewer heroic recoveries because they design fewer preventable failures. They still feel pressure, but it doesn't buckle them. They still take risks, but those risks don't erode trust. They still face a crisis, but they're structured to absorb the shock. Operational excellence is what gives them that edge, not flashy, not loud, but quietly unbreakable.

And yet, very few leaders are trained to think this way. We're taught to dream, to pitch, to scale. We're rewarded for speed, creativity, and results. But few are taught how to build systems that support those results sustainably. Few are challenged to design execution as deliberately as they create a product. Fewer still are trained to think operationally under pressure, which means the people who carry operational excellence, often unsung, often invisible, end up holding together empires of chaos without ever being given the structural authority or cultural recognition they deserve.

That has to change. And it starts by redefining what operational excellence is.

It's not efficiency for efficiency's sake. It's not running lean until something breaks. It's not putting the right people in the right seats and hoping for the best. Operational excellence is the discipline of creating systems that work at scale, under stress, and in motion. It's about building a machine that delivers reliably, not just when the founder is in the room, or the deadline is existential, or the market is favorable. But always. Cleanly. Repeatably. And with enough clarity that the organization can adapt without collapsing.

At its heart, operational excellence is not about what you do; it's about how you think. Do you value rhythm over urgency? Do you see problems such as design flaws or just execution gaps? Do you treat clarity as a leadership act or a luxury you get to later? Are you building an organization that needs heroes, or one that prevents the need for them altogether?

What follows in these pages is not a manifesto. It's a blueprint. You won't find trendy management theories or one-size-fits-all solutions. What you will find are the core disciplines that enable operational excellence to emerge and endure. We'll explore the architecture of clean execution, the layers of clarity, rhythm, resilience, feedback, and refinement that separate high-functioning organizations from brittle ones. We'll dig into case studies, not to tell stories, but to extract lessons. And we'll revisit familiar topics like roles, systems, culture, and failure, but through a lens that's grounded in operational truth, not theoretical idealism.

You'll notice something else as you read. This book isn't structured around departments or functions. That's deliberate. Operational excellence isn't confined to the ops team. It's not just for COO types or process nerds. It belongs to everyone. Product managers need it. HR teams need it. Founders need it. Customer success, finance, marketing, legal, and any function seeking to scale impact without drowning in complexity must learn to think operationally. The principles here are universal, even if the tactics vary.

But before we dive in, let's pause on a concept that will echo throughout the book. It's a simple loop, but it holds the entire discipline together. At the center of operational excellence is a cycle, a repeating rhythm of clarity, system design, disciplined execution, feedback, and adjustment. Think of it as the Operating Loop. First, you clarify intent ruthlessly. Then you design systems to deliver on that intent without relying on heroics. Next, you execute, not in manic bursts, but with clean, sustainable rhythm. You monitor for signal, detect drift early, and surface issues before they become fires. You debrief honestly, learn without blame, and adjust intelligently. And then you recommit it, not because the work is glamorous, but because excellence erodes when it's not actively maintained.

This loop isn't revolutionary. But the organizations that live it are. They don't win because they're faster or wiser. They win because they build systems that don't collapse under pressure. They create clarity where others drift. They sustain performance where others spike and crash. And they adapt in ways that are deliberate, not reactive. That's not magic. That's operational excellence in motion.

And so this book begins not with a formula, but with a challenge. Look at your organization, honestly. Strip away the surface wins, the short-term heroics, the PR gloss. What does the system look like when no one is watching? Can it deliver under stress? Can it recover from failure without losing trust? Can it scale without surrendering clarity?

If the answer is no, or not yet, you're in the right place. Because what follows isn't a playbook for perfection. It's a manual for building integrity into your operations: one decision, one system, one team at a time.

Welcome to The Book On Operational Excellence.

# Chapter 1: The Operational Excellence Imperative

There's a moment in every organization's lifespan when vision alone is no longer enough. The novelty wears off, the initial surge of momentum dissipates, and suddenly the same strategies that once propelled success begin to stall. It's not a matter of willpower, talent, or even ambition. It's the gravitational pull of execution, an invisible but unrelenting force that separates those who survive from those who quietly expire beneath the surface of complexity. Operational excellence isn't a bonus. It's the only thing keeping the walls from caving in.

At its core, operational excellence is the discipline of building an organization that performs reliably under pressure. That phrase, "performs reliably under pressure", carries more weight than it appears. It means a system that remains stable when timelines are tight, a team that doesn't disintegrate in the face of ambiguity, and a process that scales without degradation. To get there requires something more profound than playbooks and quarterly goals. It demands an entire philosophy of execution. And like any philosophy worth its salt, it needs structure.

Consider what I call the Execution Gravity Model. Imagine a constellation with three massive bodies pulling on every operational decision you make. The first is clarity, the gravitational pull of intent, direction, and purpose. Without clarity, every task becomes a drifting object, unmoored from priority or consequence. The second is precision, the requirement that execution be engineered, not improvised. Precision creates repeatability, and repeatability underwrites scale. The third force is resilience, the ability of your systems and people to bend without breaking. Clarity, accuracy, resilience: these three gravitational fields shape everything your organization does. When aligned, they create a stable orbital path that can carry velocity, weight, and change. When misaligned, you get entropy.

Let's start with a hypothetical case. A mid-stage software company, with thirty employees, has just closed Series B funding. Their product is solid, their market is warm, and the sales team has no trouble generating leads. What they can't seem to do is deliver. Sprints overrun by weeks. Client onboarding is chaotic. Internal tools crash during demos. Product updates arrive late, buggy, and without documentation. It isn't malice or laziness. It's structural entropy. No clear accountability for delivery, no sequencing of interdependencies, no rhythm of feedback to catch failures early. What this company has is an abundance of vision and a deficit of operational gravity. Clarity is missing: no shared definitions of done. Precision is absent: processes are skeletal and frequently bypassed. Resilience? Not even on the radar. When stress appears, people start improvising, and improvisation is just panic in a blazer.

Now contrast that with a real-world example from the other end of the spectrum. Toyota, particularly in the decades following World War II, is one of the clearest illustrations of operational excellence used as strategic weaponry. Faced with limited capital, restricted access to raw materials, and a domestic market still recovering from economic devastation, Toyota didn't try to outgun the giants. It redefined the rules of engagement. The Toyota Production System became legendary not because it reduced cost, it did, but because it institutionalized excellence.

14

Through concepts like jidoka (automation with a human touch) and kaizen (continuous improvement), Toyota embedded operational discipline at every layer of its system. The Andon cord, which empowered any worker to stop the assembly line if they detected an error, was not a gimmick. It was the embodiment of the idea that executional integrity mattered more than speed. That clarity of purpose, precision of method, and resilience in error correction would compound far beyond any temporary productivity gain. And it did.

So, what separates Toyota from the hypothetical tech company? It's not IQ. It's not capital. It's operational gravity. It's an organizational mass built from thousands of deliberate decisions about how work should flow, how problems should surface, and how humans should behave under stress.

Now let's dig into the failure side. Think about Blackberry. Once a dominant force in mobile communication, its market position evaporated seemingly overnight. But the collapse didn't start with marketing or strategy. It began with execution. Their processes for iterating on design were slow, siloed, and insulated from user feedback. Their operating system updates lagged far behind user expectations. They had the vision for secure enterprise communication, but lacked the operational muscle to keep pace with the market. They had ideas, but no alignment. They had urgency, but no structure. Blackberry's decline wasn't a failure of invention. It was a failure of executional adaptability, precision, and resilience, fatally misaligned.

Operational excellence doesn't mean perfection. It doesn't mean running an airtight ship at all times. What it means is predictability under complexity. It means that when something breaks, the system knows how to surface the problem without blame and fix it without delay. It means that roles, processes, and priorities are not floating guesses but nailed-down truths that can absorb pressure. It means that clarity isn't a quarterly keynote, but a daily navigational tool used by every level of the organization.

And here's the subtle truth that most leaders miss: operational excellence is not the opposite of creativity. It is the condition that enables it. When you remove uncertainty from execution, you free up attention, trust, and energy, resources that can then be spent on innovation, not survival. When people aren't wasting time triangulating ambiguous decisions, fixing broken processes, or covering for failed handoffs, they start imagining new ways forward. Creativity doesn't thrive in chaos. It thrives in coherence.

This is why the best operators aren't always the loudest. They aren't chasing flash or flair. They are tuning the machine. Quietly, methodically, relentlessly. They are embedding intelligence into the structure. They are noticing where time leaks, where communication frays, where trust erodes. And they are building environments that refuse to tolerate drift.

The Execution Gravity Model offers a diagnostic lens. When something is breaking inside your organization, projects are delayed, goals are missed, and morale is declining. Start by asking which of the three gravitational fields has weakened. Is it a clarity failure? Was the objective vague or the ownership unclear? Is it a precision failure? Were the processes ad hoc or ignored? Or is it a resilience failure? Did the system buckle when something unpredictable happened? These questions are not abstract. They are architectural. They reveal where you must reinforce.

This book begins here, at the recognition that operational excellence is not one department's job. It's not ops, IT, HR, or strategy. It is the very foundation upon which all execution stands. It is the load-bearing architecture of the entire enterprise. And like any structure designed to endure, it must be built intentionally, reinforced continually, and tested without mercy.

Operational excellence is not flashy. It will not trend on social media. But it is the quiet force that keeps great organizations from falling apart. And if you take it seriously, if you build for gravity instead of hype, you'll find that it not only holds everything together. It provides a sustainable path to accelerate your progress.

## Chapter 2: Clarity vs. Chaos in Execution

There is a certain romanticism that surrounds the idea of moving fast. In startup culture, speed is valorized almost religiously. The ability to pivot, to launch quickly, to "fail fast" is seen as a badge of strategic agility. But velocity without clarity is indistinguishable from panic. It may feel like progress, but more often than not, it's chaos dressed up in urgency. And chaos, even when self-inflicted, comes with a price.

Clarity is not about knowing everything. It's about knowing enough of the right things, at the right time, to act decisively. It's not a moral virtue or a personality trait. Clarity is operational. It is engineered. It's built into how work is initiated, how decisions are communicated, how actions are sequenced, and how feedback is metabolized. It is not a mood. It is a discipline.

To operationalize clarity, I use what I call The Clarity Chain. It is a four-link system: Intent → Translation → Execution → Feedback. It starts with the original intent, what we are trying to achieve, and why. But intent, by itself, is insufficient. It must be translated from strategic vision into operational language. That means goals become plans, plans become workflows, workflows become responsibilities. Next comes execution, doing the work with discipline and alignment. And finally, feedback, collecting, analyzing, and integrating what the execution teaches us back into our understanding of intent. When this loop is potent, clarity compounds. When any link is weak, chaos seeps in.

Let's ground this in a hypothetical example. Imagine a nonprofit organization that has found sudden success. It started with a clear mission: delivering clean water to remote communities. Donors were inspired. Volunteers were mobilized. A small team pulled off miracle projects with grit and heart. But as their visibility grew, so did the donations. Suddenly, they could scale. New staff were hired, new regions targeted, and new partnerships formed. But something shifted. Project timelines started slipping. Reporting became inconsistent. Volunteers in the field lacked key updates. Donors began to ask questions that staff couldn't answer confidently. And inside the team, morale declined. What happened?

Their intent was still noble. But the Clarity Chain fractured. The mission never translated cleanly into operational models. Field coordinators didn't know which projects took priority. Regional directors were unclear on budget constraints. Donor communication was handled reactively, not systematically. And because the organization lacked structured feedback loops, early warning signs were missed. The entire operation began to suffer, not from bad people or bad ideas, but from unmanaged ambiguity. The speed of growth overwhelmed the clarity of execution.

Now contrast that with Toyota's legendary Andon cord, a simple device with profound implications. On Toyota's factory floor, any worker at any station has the authority to pull a cord that stops the entire production line if they observe a defect. To an outsider, that may seem risky or even wasteful. Why halt a multi-million-dollar process for a single missed step? But in practice, it is the purest form of executive clarity.

The Andon cord embodies all four links in the Clarity Chain. The intent, zero defects and continuous improvement, is well understood. It is translated into the operational norm that quality trumps speed. Workers are trained not just in how to do their jobs but in what the organization values. The execution is disciplined: every movement, every process, is tightly choreographed but flexible when deviation is needed. And most crucially, the feedback is immediate. A line stop isn't a failure; it's an information event. It signals where the system needs reinforcement. This is not clarity as abstraction. It is clarity as embodied infrastructure.

Toyota's system is slow only when it needs to be. Paradoxically, it is this engineered willingness to stop that allows the organization to move faster over time. By preventing minor errors from compounding into large ones, by creating a culture where anyone can act decisively in the name of quality, they build operational trust. That trust, in turn, accelerates decision-making and reduces the cognitive drag of ambiguity.

This is where many fast-moving organizations stumble. In the rush to maintain momentum, they skip over translation. They assume everyone "gets it." But assumptions breed misalignment. A founder articulates a compelling strategy at the all-hands meeting, and two weeks later, her team is pursuing five different interpretations of that strategy. Not because they're insubordinate, but because the strategy wasn't translated into specific executional guidance. How does this affect priorities? What gets postponed? Who makes the trade-off when two deadlines collide?

Translation is the bridge between clarity and motion. And it's often the missing piece.

Consider the startup world. Many teams pride themselves on being "scrappy" and "lean." What that often means is unstructured. The first dozen hires figure things out on the fly. There are no process owners, no defined escalation paths, and no shared language for when to intervene. Everyone is moving fast, and everyone is interpreting the mission in slightly different ways. For a time, it works. Until it doesn't. Until one hand doesn't know what the other is building, and suddenly they've shipped features that can't integrate, created campaigns that contradict, or burned out their talent with endless pivots. The irony is that what they thought was speed was fragmentation. The absence of clarity did not accelerate them. It just hid the cost until it became unaffordable.

And yet, clarity isn't the enemy of speed. It's how speed becomes sustainable. A team that knows exactly what matters, what to do next, and how to escalate problems isn't slow. They're liberated. They don't waste time second-guessing. They don't fight internal battles over priorities. They execute. They adapt with alignment, not improvisation.

Here's a concrete pattern I've seen across dozens of operational turnarounds: when clarity improves, friction drops. When friction drops, trust increases. And when trust increases, the speed of work accelerates without burnout. This is the compounding effect of operational clarity. It builds alignment not as a one-time achievement, but as a dynamic loop that improves the more you invest in it.

Let's return to the nonprofit example. Their recovery didn't come from more staff or more funding. It came from slowing down long enough to rebuild their Clarity Chain. They redefined what success meant per region. They documented workflows. They created feedback loops that involved both field staff and donors. They developed a shared cadence of reporting and decisions. Within a year, the noise diminished. Projects began to land on time. Donors felt reconnected. The mission had not changed, but the path to executing it became visible.

That's what clarity does. It makes alignment visible. It makes ambiguity addressable. It makes complexity manageable. And in a world that will only grow more volatile, that kind of clarity isn't optional. It's armor.

Clarity is not a moment. It is not a memo. It is not a motivational speech. It is a chain of decisions, reinforcements, and reflections. If any link is weak, the system suffers. If all links are strong, the organization becomes unstoppable, not because it's rushing, but because it's coordinated. Because the people inside it don't just work hard, they work together, towards the same thing, in the same direction, at the same time.

And that is the true opposite of chaos. Not rigidity. Not slowness. But disciplined coherence. When clarity reigns, execution becomes art. Not because it's flashy, but because it holds.

# Chapter 3: Beyond Efficiency – The Systemic Lens

Efficiency, for all its appeal, is often a dangerous seduction. It promises leaner operations, faster cycles, and reduced waste. But pursued too early or in isolation, efficiency becomes a liability. It pressures teams to streamline processes that were never structurally sound to begin with. It reinforces performance theater over system truth. And perhaps most dangerously, it conceals fragility behind metrics that temporarily look better, until they don't.

Operational excellence isn't about maximizing output per unit of time. It's about building systems that can execute reliably under stress, at scale, and over time. That reliability doesn't come from working harder. It comes from designing execution as a system, a coherent, adaptive, self-correcting loop. At the heart of that loop lies what I call the Systemic Leverage Map, a framework composed of four critical components: Inputs, Flow, Feedback, and Correction. This model is less about tactics and more about architecture—each link in this chain either compounds clarity or leaks entropy. And when leaders fail to see the whole loop, when they optimize one node at the expense of the others, they end up solving the wrong problem with the wrong tools.

The first point of leverage in any system is its inputs. These are the raw materials of execution: the data we rely on, the goals we set, the decisions we feed into the process. If those inputs are misaligned, no amount of downstream optimization will save you. I worked with a mid-sized hospital that was facing chronic bottlenecks in emergency care. Administrators blamed slow triage, outdated infrastructure, and even staff morale. But the root problem was upstream: intake forms were incomplete, patient symptoms were misclassified, and key details were lost between handoffs. The flow wasn't broken; the inputs were. They were trying to build operational speed on top of corrupted data. After restructuring their intake protocol to include clear categories, digitizing critical fields, and embedding quick checkpoints, the system's downstream processes began to flow more cleanly. It wasn't about doing things faster. It was about starting from a place of accuracy and intent.

But clean inputs mean little if the flow of execution is incoherent. Flow is where most organizations quietly lose time, energy, and trust. It's how work moves from one step to the next, how decisions pass between people, how tasks surface, transfer, and resolve. When flow is designed poorly, when it's based on informal knowledge, historical quirks, or personal preference, people start to improvise. They build workarounds, over-communicate, second-guess, and eventually burn out. This isn't a matter of laziness or attitude. It's what happens when a system resists its users.

I witnessed this phenomenon in a nonprofit that had rapidly scaled following a viral fundraising campaign. They added programs, regions, and staff, but not operational flow. Their internal systems were duct-taped together: donor data was stored in spreadsheets, program updates were shared via Slack, and approvals were stuck in email threads. The result wasn't visible chaos; it was slow-drip misalignment. Teams launched redundant projects. Donors received inconsistent updates. Staff began to disengage, not because they didn't care, but because they couldn't see how their work connected to the whole. They moved fast, but nothing flowed. It wasn't until the organization paused and mapped its workflows — specifically, who handed off to whom, what tools carried the work, and where decisions got stuck — that real flow began to emerge. And with that, performance accelerated, not because people were trying harder, but because the system was finally supporting them.

Still, flow without feedback is directionless. Feedback is what tells a system whether it's working. Without it, organizations lose their ability to detect errors, measure success, or adapt. Yet in many companies, feedback is treated as a quarterly event or a reactive panic response. Systems that excel embed feedback loops directly into their architecture. Feedback isn't something you schedule. It's something the system produces, continuously and without ego.

A public school district I worked with had invested heavily in new curriculum tools, hoping to improve classroom engagement. But months into rollout, adoption lagged and learning outcomes flatlined. The tools weren't inherently flawed, but the feedback system was. Teachers had no formal process for reporting what worked, what didn't, or what broke down during lesson delivery. Product updates were top-down and out of sync with field reality. Feedback existed, but it was unstructured and emotionally loaded, passed informally or withheld altogether. After installing lightweight weekly feedback rituals, anonymous inputs, quick reflection loops, and targeted escalation paths, patterns began to emerge. Minor bugs got fixed before they became chronic. Teachers felt heard. System updates became grounded in use, not assumption. Feedback didn't just improve morale; it transformed the system from a rigid deployment into an evolving architecture.

But even feedback is insufficient without correction. Feedback tells you what happened. Correction is what you do about it. And this is where most systems quietly fail. They treat insights as informational, not actionable. Or they rely on individual initiative to act, rather than embedding correction as a system-level behavior. In operationally excellent systems, correction isn't a fire drill; it's a loop. It happens early, frequently, and without shame.

Take the example of a large logistics firm implementing AI-powered route optimization. Their initial deployment showed promising projections on paper: lower fuel use, faster delivery times, fewer human decisions. But in the field, drivers began to ignore the routing engine. They rerouted themselves, quietly and frequently. The AI model didn't factor in local realities, such as unplowed roads, known warehouse delays, and unmarked construction. Drivers had institutional memory that the system lacked. At first, leadership assumed resistance. But when they shadowed the process, they discovered a simple truth: the system needed a correction loop. They built a feedback capture layer into the driver app, then trained the model weekly with real-world routing adjustments. Over time, route accuracy increased. But more importantly, the system began to learn. The correction wasn't reactive. It became a design layer.

The lesson here isn't just that Inputs, Flow, Feedback, and Correction matter. It's that they are interdependent. Weakness in one creates drag in all. Clean inputs without precise flow still yield confusion. Elegant flow without feedback leads to delusion.

Feedback without correction yields cynicism. And correction without structural redesign creates burnout.

The organizations that build operational excellence at scale aren't the ones that master one domain of execution. They're the ones that build whole-system awareness. They don't chase surface efficiency. They pursue structural clarity. They don't just speed up what they already do. They ask whether the system itself makes sense.

Efficiency, in that context, becomes the byproduct of a coherent system, not the goal. And that's the difference between operations that shine briefly and those that endure. Not how quickly they move, but how cleanly they operate.

# Chapter 4: Foundations of Repeatable Excellence

Every organization eventually confronts the limits of effort. Early wins come from talent, improvisation, and grit. But as systems grow more complex and the stakes increase, individual heroics start to break down. People can't carry the execution on their backs forever. Talent may still be exceptional, but outcomes become inconsistent. What once felt sharp and decisive begins to wobble. Quality drifts. Deadlines slip. Institutional memory fades. And the same work that once felt energizing becomes exhausting, not because the mission changed, but because the system never matured.

This is the moment where repeatable excellence becomes not just valuable, but essential. It's the shift from heroism to architecture, from ad hoc brilliance to designed reliability. It's not about stripping autonomy. It's about building infrastructure, operational scaffolding that lets the average team member deliver above-average results, repeatedly, even under pressure.

At the heart of this shift is what I call the **Repeatability Stack**, a layered model for operational resilience. It consists of four interdependent layers: **Process, Principle, People, and Platform**. Each layer plays a distinct role in translating potential into consistent performance. And each, if neglected, introduces variability that compounds over time.

The foundation is **Process**, the structured sequencing of how work gets done. Done well, the process eliminates ambiguity. It transforms intuition into instruction. It stores knowledge in the system, not in individuals. But the process is not a checklist. It's a mechanism for converting experience into guidance. Without it, every outcome is a coin toss.

Stacked above the process is Principle, the values and heuristics that govern when to follow the process and when to adapt. Principles guide judgment. They prevent rigidity. They help teams resolve trade-offs without needing constant supervision. In moments of uncertainty, principles are what align decentralized decisions with organizational intent.

Next is **People**, not just talent, but clarity of role, cross-functionality, and operational maturity. People make the system breathe. But their effectiveness depends on how clearly they understand their position in the stack. In systems without clear roles, even great performers create confusion. Alignment becomes personality-dependent. Resilience becomes luck.

And finally, at the top, is **Platform**, the tools, systems, and digital infrastructure that operationalize the other layers. Platforms are the scale engine. They enable well-designed processes to run faster, principles to be integrated into workflows, and people to work without being overwhelmed by coordination overhead. Platform isn't just software, it's system architecture. And when it's well integrated, it creates leverage without introducing drag.

To see how these layers interact, consider the example of onboarding a new hire. Onboarding is a deceptively simple task that quickly reveals the strength, or fragility, of your Repeatability Stack.

Imagine a fast-growing product company bringing in a new QA engineer. On day one, the process layer should provide a clear, sequenced path: environment setup, tool access, intro meetings, workflow overview, testing protocols. But process alone isn't enough. Suppose the product is at a mid-pivot point and the existing documentation doesn't fully apply. That's where principle comes in: the new hire is taught to prioritize user-impacting regressions over edge cases, and to escalate when clarity is missing. These principles give them freedom within form.

As the engineer begins real work, the people layer activates. Their mentor, another QA lead, isn't just a buddy. They have defined responsibilities: checking the new hire's early work, answering domain-specific questions, and flagging systemic gaps in onboarding content. The product team, meanwhile, knows when and how to loop QA into release cycles, because roles and handoffs are mapped.

Finally, the platform layer ties it together. Access to testing tools is automated through provisioning scripts. The onboarding checklist lives in a shared system that tracks progress and surfaces blockers. The bug tracking platform already reflects company-wide testing priorities through tag templates aligned with the principles. Nothing has to be reinvented.

Now imagine what happens when one of these layers fails.

If the process is undocumented, the new hire wastes time asking the same questions five predecessors asked. If principles are absent, they may test in ways that technically follow procedure but miss product risk. If people's roles are unclear, feedback arrives too late, and the engineer floats without calibration. And if the platform is misaligned, basic tasks, such as submitting bugs, escalating issues, and tracking test coverage, become sources of friction rather than flow.

The system doesn't collapse all at once. But performance becomes noisy. Work slows. Trust erodes. And instead of compounding capability, the organization begins to leak energy.

That's why excellence must be architected, not assumed. When all four layers of the Repeatability Stack align, systems absorb complexity without losing clarity. Teams don't just perform well once; they do it again and again, even when the context changes. That's what operational maturity looks like. Not brilliance in moments, but consistency across them.

The organizations that endure are not those that hope for heroism. They are the ones that make excellence repeatable, not by controlling every variable, but by designing an environment where success is the default outcome, not the exception.

# Chapter 5: Friction and Flow

There's a form of organizational drag that doesn't make headlines or show up on dashboards, but compounds quietly, relentlessly. It isn't dramatic. It's subtle. It's the friction that accumulates across decisions, handoffs, tools, and processes. It's the time lost waiting for approvals, the energy drained navigating broken systems, the talent misused on workarounds that shouldn't exist in the first place. Friction isn't just inconvenient, it's corrosive. It bleeds morale, slows momentum, and erodes trust in the system itself.

What makes friction dangerous is its invisibility. It rarely looks like failure. It presents as an inconvenience, a harmless delay, or process quirks that everyone learns to work around. But over time, that tolerance becomes cultural. Teams stop asking why things are slow. They accept drag as usual. And when that happens, excellence becomes not just difficult, but unsustainable.

Diagnosing friction requires more than gut instinct. It demands structure. That's where the **Operational Flow Audit** comes in. It's a framework designed to surface where execution gets blocked, not through abstract models, but through a simple, targeted lens: Time, Talent, and Tools. Time measures where delays compound. Talent assesses whether skills are misapplied. Tools evaluate whether systems support or sabotage flow. Taken together, these three dimensions reveal how work moves, or fails to.

The first layer is Time. Not just the total time a task takes, but the hidden delays between steps. These are the lags that accumulate in silos, approvals, unclear ownership, and asynchronous workflows. A mid-sized law firm once implemented a sleek new billing platform to improve invoicing efficiency. But within weeks, billing cycles had slowed rather than accelerated. The root cause wasn't the tool; it was the approval process. Every invoice above a certain threshold required sign-off from a senior partner, a person whose calendar was perpetually overloaded. Invoices sat in digital purgatory for days. No one challenged the policy because it had never been operationally audited. Once surfaced, the firm restructured approvals with tiered thresholds and delegated authority. What had felt like a tool problem was a time design flaw.

Next is Talent. This is where friction hides in misalignment, people doing work they're overqualified for, duplicating efforts, or spinning in ambiguity. In an extensive public high school system, administrative staff were routinely buried in manual data entry tasks. Attendance records, scheduling overrides, and special accommodations are all handled by hand. These weren't trivial roles. These were experienced coordinators who knew how to resolve student crises, manage disciplinary pathways, and support complex family dynamics. But they spent most of their time clicking through outdated interfaces and correcting spreadsheet errors introduced upstream. When the district ran a flow audit, they found that just 30% of staff time was spent on core responsibilities. The fix wasn't hiring more people. It was aligning existing talent with high-leverage work by redesigning input accuracy, creating shared databases, and removing redundant tracking layers. The staff didn't change. The system did.

Then come Tools. Technology, when misaligned, amplifies friction instead of reducing it. Organizations often accumulate tools without a strategy, each one solving a localized problem but creating systemic dissonance. A well-funded tech startup once prided itself on its tool stack. They used five platforms for task management, three communication channels, and two knowledge bases. But nothing integrated cleanly. Meeting notes were manually copied across different tools. Tasks lived in multiple systems with inconsistent labels. Status updates had to be broadcast redundantly because there was no single source of truth. People didn't resist tools; they resisted noise. A flow audit revealed that 40% of their team's time was spent either syncing between tools or recovering from miscommunication caused by that sync failing. By consolidating their systems, establishing a clear hierarchy of tools, and building training around that structure, they didn't just move faster; they moved with less friction.

These three categories — Time, Talent, Tools — are not exhaustive, but they offer a reliable diagnostic base. They provide organizations with a way to interrogate their systems without resorting to blame or burnout. When you look at execution through this lens, you start to notice the difference between resistance caused by workload and resistance caused by system design.

I once worked with a manufacturing plant where production delays were blamed on equipment maintenance. The assumption was simple: machines were old; they needed replacement. But a flow audit told a different story. The delays weren't mechanical; they were procedural. Maintenance logs were paper-based, stored offsite, and updated weekly. Line managers had to wait hours, sometimes days, to verify part availability or track pending work orders. Skilled operators spent downtime chasing information instead of solving problems. The system wasn't broken because of equipment; it was broken because of information flow. They digitized the maintenance process, linked it to inventory in real time, and embedded alerts directly into the line manager's dashboard. The machines didn't change. The data did. And with it, flow returned.

Friction isn't always fixable at once. But once made visible, it becomes addressable. And the most telling signal of operational maturity is how seriously an organization treats its hidden drag. High-functioning systems aren't the ones that never face friction. They're the ones that catch it early, name it clearly, and design it out repeatedly.

The goal of operational design isn't perfection. It's flow. Not just smoother movement, but lighter movement. Systems that enable people to focus more on value and less on resistance. When Time, Talent, and Tools align, work doesn't just get done, it moves with rhythm, clarity, and trust.

That's not efficiency. That's operational clarity in motion. And once you feel it, once a team starts operating without the constant tax of friction, you stop tolerating the weight. You start designing for the work to move.

# Chapter 6: Excellence as an Ecosystem

Operational excellence rarely fails in isolation. It fails at the seams, where departments meet but don't communicate, where tools clash with culture, where pace outstrips process, or where well-meaning people work at cross-purposes under the illusion of progress. It's not enough to have great teams or solid systems. What determines lasting excellence is whether those elements cohere into an ecosystem, interdependent, adaptive, and aligned.

That's the paradox: your organization might be full of smart people, doing their jobs well, and still be failing. Because excellence isn't additive, it's systemic. It's not about isolated brilliance. It's about orchestration.

At the core of this orchestration is what I call the Execution Ecosystem Model. It aligns three elements: Culture, Tools, and Tempo. Culture is how people think and behave under pressure. Tools are the systems they use to act. Tempo is the cadence at which decisions are made and operations executed. Misalignment between any two of these creates drag. Misalignment across all three creates chaos.

Start with a hypothetical: a mid-sized school district in a diverse urban area. They've made enormous investments in teacher training. Their faculty includes former industry professionals, award-winning educators, and deeply committed mentors. Students love them. Parents respect them. On paper, instructional excellence is high.

But under the surface, the scheduling system is broken. Classrooms are double-booked. Lunch periods overlap with elective blocks. Some teachers don't get assigned rooms until two weeks into the semester. The transportation system, managed by a separate department, routinely drops students off late. IT support is reactive, not proactive; online learning platforms crash during high-stakes assessments. Everyone's working hard, but nothing flows—and morale sinks, not because of bad teaching, but because the operational backbone is cracked. The culture values excellence, but the tools and tempo betray it.

This is the danger of fragmented execution. Culture without tools is frustration. Tools without culture are bureaucracy. Tempo without either is burnout. Excellence only emerges when all three align and reinforce each other.

Now consider Apple. Much has been said about its sleek designs, its product secrecy, and its marketing brilliance. But behind all of that is one of the most tightly integrated operational ecosystems in the modern world. Apple doesn't just make beautiful products; it builds systems in which every element, from industrial design to component sourcing to retail execution, is choreographed like a symphony.

Take the iPhone. Design begins not with aesthetics alone, but with a deep integration between what's possible in materials science, chip architecture, and manufacturing constraints. Hardware engineers collaborate directly with software teams to ensure performance and user experience align. Supply chain teams are looped in early to guarantee that design decisions don't create downstream bottlenecks. Retail staff are trained not just to sell but to explain features in a language that echoes design philosophy. Culture, tools, and tempo are aligned. That's not accidental. That's ecosystem-level thinking.

And it pays. Apple's ability to launch products globally, with synchronized supply and seamless user experience, isn't just a function of budget. It's the result of refusing to let excellence live in silos.

By contrast, I once advised a fast-scaling fintech startup with a brilliant data science team. Their fraud detection models were top-tier, far superior to industry benchmarks. But those models sat idle for months. Why? The product team struggled to integrate them into the app flow because they didn't understand how to do so. The customer support team had no idea the feature existed. And the executive team, chasing rapid expansion, deprioritized internal alignment. What could've been a strategic advantage became a sunk cost. Culture was curious and innovative. Tools were powerful. But tempo was misaligned, too fast to allow for cross-functional synthesis.

This is the failure pattern of the modern operator: mistaking local wins for global progress. You can't build an organization like a Lego tower, stacking departments on top of each other and hoping they click. You have to design it like an ecosystem, interdependent, self-regulating, and responsive to feedback.

The Execution Ecosystem Model begins with a question: Where is misalignment costing you the most? Sometimes it's cultural values written on the wall but ignored in meetings. Sometimes it's technological, legacy systems duct-taped to modern workflows. Sometimes it's temporal, teams moving at different speeds, creating friction at every interface. To fix it, you don't start with directives. You begin by listening. Where do people feel stuck? Where are decisions slow? Where do tools feel imposed, not empowering?

I saw this play out with a logistics company trying to upgrade its routing software. The tech team built a powerful optimization engine. But the dispatchers ignored it. Why? Because it didn't reflect local knowledge. It rerouted trucks without accounting for relationships with warehouse staff or the reliability of specific shortcuts. The tool had technical excellence but cultural dissonance. So adoption failed, and morale suffered. The problem wasn't resistance to change; it was the absence of ecosystem design.

Success, in contrast, feels like seamlessness, not in the sense of perfection, but of alignment. When culture, tools, and tempo reinforce each other, operations breathe. Information flows where it's needed. Teams act without waiting for permission. Problems surface early. Feedback loops close fast.

You can feel it. In meetings that run on time and end with clarity. In handoffs that don't require translation. In launches that don't melt down in the final stretch. This is what operational health looks like, not just speed, but coherence.

The metaphor here isn't machinery. It's biology. Healthy ecosystems don't grow by force. They grow through balance, interdependence, and adaptability. Remove a predator, and prey populations explode. Introduce a new species, and old ones migrate. The same dynamics play out in your organization. Overinvest in tools without cultural readiness, and you get resistance. Push tempo without clarity, and you get mistakes. Over-focus on culture without supporting systems, and you get burnout masked as passion.

So take inventory. Where is your excellence isolated rather than integrated? Where do your best teams feel most disconnected? Where are good ideas dying in the gap between departments?

That's where the work begins, not in optimizing individual parts, but in designing for interdependence.

Because operational excellence isn't a product of effort alone, it's the outcome of alignment. Culture, tools, and tempo, when they move together, create not just better results, but a better way to work. One where teams feel the lift, not just the load. One where success doesn't require heroics, just harmony.

That's the goal. Not to build faster. Not to make louder. But to build together. Because in the end, the organizations that win aren't the ones with the best parts. They're the ones with the best orchestration.

# Chapter 7: Architecture as Leverage

Architecture isn't just what holds the walls up. It's what shapes how people move through them. In an organization, architecture isn't made of steel and concrete; it's composed of objectives, processes, systems, and the constraints that bind them. But the effect is the same: it governs behavior. Whether people collaborate or isolate, improvise or execute with precision, take ownership or defer, these aren't merely personality traits. They are architectural responses.

Most leaders don't think this way. They build roles, teams, and tool stacks the way people add furniture to a room, based on availability, urgency, or taste. They grow by addition, not by design. The result is an organization that feels more like a warehouse than a blueprint. Lots of stuff. No structural logic.

But when architecture is intentional, it becomes leverage. It lets you scale without friction, adapt without panic, and operate with far less management overhead. That's where the OPS/ARC framework comes in. On one side, you define your Objectives, the Processes that drive them, and the Systems that support them. On the other side, you design for Agility, Redundancy, and Constraints, the architectural principles that determine how the organization behaves under pressure.

Let's begin with a hypothetical. A boutique marketing agency, successful and growing fast. They start with five people, founder-led, tight-knit, high-energy. Clients love them. Referrals pour in. Within eighteen months, they doubled their team. Then double again. But something cracks. Deadlines slip. Campaigns go live with typos. Internal edits get lost. Designers don't know who owns the brief. Developers don't know who signed off. Tension rises.

It's not a talent issue. They've hired smart people. But their operational architecture hasn't evolved. The objective is still clear: deliver high-quality campaigns on time. But their processes were built for a five-person team and haven't scaled. They rely on Slack threads instead of structured project management. Approvals live in email inboxes. Creative briefs vary wildly in format. And worst of all, their tool stack has become a Frankenstein's monster of overlapping apps, with each person using what they prefer, resulting in no single source of truth.

Their failure isn't operational; it's architectural. They've added people without redesigning the structure. Their agility has turned into chaos. There's no redundancy, only single points of failure. And their constraints are accidental, not designed.

Now contrast that with Shopify. From the beginning, Shopify built its operational architecture like a platform, not a product. As it grew from a simple e-commerce tool into a commerce operating system, its underlying structure enabled, rather than resisted, scale. Merchants didn't just get a storefront; they got plug-and-play APIs, theming frameworks, and integrations with thousands of apps. Internally, Shopify mirrored that modularity. Teams could ship features independently without breaking the system. Objectives were clear: empower merchants. Processes reflected that they reduce time-to-deploy and prioritize extensibility. Systems supported it: internal developer tools, strong CI/CD pipelines, and layered access control.

And the ARC side? Agility was baked in through modular deployment. Redundancy existed at every layer, from data to personnel. Constraints weren't obstacles; they were guides. Teams couldn't launch products that violated platform conventions. That constraint prevented entropy. It kept the ecosystem clean.

This is what it looks like when architecture becomes leverage. You don't manage complexity, you absorb it. You don't slow down with scale; you get sharper. The system teaches itself to adapt.

Let's break down the OPS/ARC model more precisely.

Start with Objectives. This isn't about slogans. It's about alignment. Does your organization know what it's trying to achieve? Do teams have clarity on which outcomes matter most? If your objectives aren't architected, your processes will drift and your systems will calcify in the wrong shape.

Then come Processes. These are the arteries of your operation. But they need to be both durable and editable. Durable, so people don't reinvent the wheel. Editable, allowing people to evolve them as context shifts. Processes that are too rigid become bottlenecks. Too loose, and they dissolve into anarchy.

Then Systems. Tools are only as powerful as the way they're used. What are your systems optimizing for? Visibility? Speed? Control? Interoperability? Your systems should reflect your objectives and reinforce your processes. When they don't, friction creeps in—duplication multiplies. And the system becomes an enemy of the goal.

Now to the architectural triad: Agility, Redundancy, and Constraints.

Agility is not speed. It's responsiveness without drama. Can your teams shift priorities without spiraling into chaos? Do they know how to make decisions when plans change? Agility is built through practice, but it's enabled by architecture—cross-functional visibility. Clear escalation paths. Slack in the right places.

Redundancy isn't a waste. It's resilience. In great architecture, no single failure collapses the system. That means cross-training. Documented processes. Multiple data backups. When the lead account manager is sick, the client doesn't suffer. That's architectural foresight.

Constraints, finally, are what give form. The mistake most leaders make is treating constraints as threats to creativity. But architecture without constraint is a ruin. You need rules. Not control rules, but alignment rules. No feature gets shipped without QA. No design leaves the studio without copy reviewed. No budget is approved without a business case. These are not bureaucratic rituals; they're scaffolding.

You see the difference between ad hoc structure and adaptive architecture most clearly in stress. Back to the marketing agency. When their biggest client threatened to walk, they scrambled. They held late-night calls. Built a last-minute dashboard. Moved creatives off other projects. They delivered. But at what cost? Burnout. Resentment. Sloppy handoffs elsewhere. They survived the test, but barely.

Shopify, on the other hand, has weathered platform outages, product pivots, and global supply chain crises by leaning into architecture. When a core API failed during peak traffic, systems rerouted traffic. Teams knew precisely where to look. Recovery happened in hours, not days. Not because people were superheroes, but because the architecture absorbed the shock.

This is the ultimate lever of operational excellence: systems that hold their shape under stress. Not brittle. Not bloated. But elastic and elegant.

The question every operator must ask is: What shape is your organization? Are you designing it? Or are you just reacting to it?

Because every day, whether you realize it or not, your organization is being shaped. By how meetings are run. By which tools are used. By what gets documented. By what goes unsaid. Architecture is always happening. The only choice is whether it's happening by design or by default.

And if you want leverage, real, durable, compounding leverage, you build that architecture deliberately. You stop solving problems in isolation and start solving for structure.

You begin to see that your job isn't to fix fires. The goal is to build a system that prevents fires from spreading. That's what architecture does. It doesn't prevent failure. But it prevents collapse.

And that's what makes it leverage, not because it makes everything perfect. But because it makes everything possible.

# Chapter 8: The Discipline of Process Clarity

It starts with a sigh. A confused glance. A Slack message that reads, "Who do I ask about this?" No one panics. No one screams. But under the surface, something critical is breaking down: trust in the system. Not trust in people, necessarily, but in the invisible structure meant to carry the work forward. That fracture begins the moment process clarity erodes. And it spreads fast.

Organizations often mistake documented procedures for clarity. But true process clarity isn't about documentation. It's about operational exactness. Not the number of steps listed, but whether they align with lived experience. Whether they reduce uncertainty. Whether they let a person move from task to decision without fear, they've missed something crucial.

The workplace is filled with frustration, not because people don't want to do good work, but because they're asked to guess. Guess what matters. Guess who owns what. Guess when it's done. When you ask for excellence but give ambiguity, you don't get creativity; you get anxiety.

This is why we need the Process Precision Pyramid, a simple framework built around three critical layers: Scope, Sequence, and Signals. Get these wrong, and even talented people stall. Get them right, and average people outperform expectations.

Let's start with a hypothetical. A mid-sized tech company hires a new operations manager. Bright, eager, with experience in logistics. Her job is to streamline internal vendor onboarding. She's told: "Make it smoother, less red tape." She's been introduced to a few department heads, granted access to the

CRM, and received the last manager's notes, which are scattered and half outdated: no formal kickoff, no defined success metrics. By week three, she's buried in exceptions and angry emails. By week five, she's second-guessing her every move. By week eight, she's burned out. Not because she couldn't handle the work. But because the process failed her.

There was no Scope, no precise boundary of what success looked like, what she owned, or where her job ended and someone else's began. There was no Sequence, no standard order of operations, no step-by-step logic for how vendors were selected, entered, approved, or activated. And there were no Signals, no reliable indicators to show progress, completion, or escalation. She wasn't set up to succeed. She was set up to improvise. And improvisation without context becomes chaos.

Now, contrast that with UPS. For decades, their logistics playbook has been regarded as operational gospel. But nowhere is their obsession with process clarity more vivid than in how they train and support drivers. Every route is engineered down to left-turn minimization. Trucks are packed in reverse delivery order. Drivers are trained not just on routes but on how to step out of the car, how to hold the package, and how to confirm delivery. Why? Because precision at scale compounds. One unnecessary turn, one inefficient package placement, one delay in locating an address, multiplied across millions of deliveries, costs time, money, and morale.

Their process clarity isn't just about speed. It's about confidence. A driver who knows the sequence, trusts the signals, and understands their scope doesn't hesitate. They don't waste time wondering if they've missed something. They move. That momentum, the ability to act without rechecking everything, is not personality. It's architecture.

So, let's go deeper into the Process Precision Pyramid.

Scope is the outer shell. It defines the process, including where it starts and ends. When the scope is unclear, people duplicate effort, miss handoffs, or ignore edge cases. A simple example: If a customer refund process doesn't define when finance takes over from support, you'll get customers who wait days for resolution, or worse, get conflicting answers. Scope is the answer to the question: What's mine to own?

Sequence is the operational skeleton. It determines the order in which things must happen to avoid errors. It answers: What comes next? In what order? For what reason? Sequence is often where organizations try to get creative, and that's dangerous. There are moments for innovation. But sequence is where you protect coherence. The failure to sequence creates loops that never close. Consider a scenario where HR conducts interviews with candidates before the hiring manager has had a chance to review the role profile. Or an engineering team merging code before QA signs off. Sequence is where discipline lives.

Signals are the living pulse of the process. They tell you where you are, what's done, what's pending, and what's broken. They answer: How do I know when I've succeeded? Who gets notified? What does "done" actually mean? In systems with poor signaling, work feels endless. People recheck, revalidate, and resend. In clear systems, work has shape. It ends cleanly. Feedback loops close.

Think about how much workplace frustration traces back to missing one of these three. A handoff that never happened?

Signal failure. A task repeated by two people? Scope confusion. A critical review was skipped? Sequence error.

And consider the emotional cost. Process clarity doesn't just improve output; it changes how people feel about their work. A new hire with a precise onboarding sequence moves from apprehension to confidence. A sales team with a defined pitch-to-close pipeline moves from improvisation to rhythm. A developer with a transparent code review path feels empowered, not second-guessed.

The gap between "do your best" and "here's the play" is not about micromanagement. It's about trust. Trust that the system will support good work. Trust that following the process leads to success. Trust that ambiguity won't punish effort.

The most dangerous myth in operations is that clarity kills creativity. The truth is the opposite. Clarity unlocks creativity by removing the fear of missing something. When people don't have to double-check everything, they can think bigger. Move faster. Ship smarter.

But there's a caveat. Clarity has to live, not just exist. A process written in a PDF and buried in SharePoint doesn't create clarity. It establishes false confidence. For process clarity to work, it must be visible, accessible, and updated. It must reflect how work gets done, not how it got done five org-charts ago.

Here's where many companies go wrong. They treat the process like a compliance checkbox. "It's documented" becomes the end of the conversation. But clarity is a living relationship between people and systems. It needs feedback. It needs iteration. It needs stewards.

When I worked with a fintech firm struggling with onboarding delays, we didn't start by rewriting procedures. We began by shadowing the process and observing where people encountered obstacles, where they asked for help. Where they took shortcuts. And what we saw was revealing: the formal process had twelve steps. The actual process involved twenty-two individuals, most of whom were undocumented. People had created workarounds, email chains, side chats, and even a Google Doc that functioned as the unofficial source of truth.

The fix wasn't a better checklist. It was alignment. Bringing the real sequence into view. Tightening scope. Embedding signals into their tools, automatic status changes, Slack triggers, and dashboards with red-yellow-green indicators.

Within weeks, completion times dropped by 40%. Not because people worked harder, but because they stopped guessing.

This is what operational clarity offers: not control, but freedom. Not rigidity, but reliability. And not just efficiency, but trust.

So, the next time a project goes sideways, don't just ask who missed what. Ask what part of the pyramid collapsed. Was the scope misaligned? Was the sequence broken? Were the signals missing?

Because the difference between floundering and flourishing often comes down to this: do your people know the play? Or are they playing by feel, in the dark?

In the end, clarity is not about perfection. It's about confidence. Not that everything will go right, but that when things go wrong, the path back is clear.

# Chapter 9: Executional Integrity

Executional integrity doesn't collapse suddenly. It erodes, quietly, incrementally, structurally. Most organizational failures don't come from laziness or malice. They come from tolerance. A missed checkpoint here. A fuzzy handoff there. A goal that's redefined after the fact, a metric that's adjusted quietly, a problem noticed but unspoken. It all adds up. And by the time the system buckles, the root issue isn't incompetence. It's the long-neglected absence of operational truth.

We often talk about integrity in moral terms, honesty, character, and ethics. But in operations, integrity is mechanical. It's about alignment between what's said and what's done, between intent and execution. It's whether a system behaves the way it claims to. Whether the loop between commitment, measurement, correction, and reflection is functional or performative.

Few stories illustrate the cost of broken integrity more starkly than Boeing's 737 Max crisis. Pressured to compete with Airbus and eager to promise a fuel-efficient aircraft that wouldn't require retraining pilots, Boeing made a series of decisions that compromised execution at nearly every level. Known issues with the MCAS system were downplayed. Internal concerns were buried beneath schedule pressure. Simulations were passed with minimal scrutiny. When the crashes occurred, the tragedy was not in the malfunction alone; it was in the system that allowed it to persist unchecked.

But as crucial as this example is, it's easy to view it as exceptional, massive, corporate, and distant. Integrity failures, though, are not limited to aviation or multinational firms. They play out in smaller, quieter ways every day, which is why it's equally important to examine moments where executional integrity was held, where it was preserved, not through perfection, but through design.

Several years ago, a fast-growing B2B software company faced a difficult product decision. A flagship release was behind schedule. Clients were anticipating the launch, marketing had already announced the timeline, and internal teams were under pressure to "make it happen." During a routine pre-release audit, a mid-level QA engineer identified a subtle yet critical issue: a performance degradation in legacy environments that hadn't been part of the core test suite. The problem wasn't fatal, but it introduced risk, particularly for a few high-value clients still on older infrastructure.

Leadership had a choice: ship now and patch later, or delay. The easy path was clear. The smart path was more challenging. But the company had built its operational integrity deliberately. They had embedded correction rights deep into the workflow. The QA team had escalation protocols that didn't require political capital. The release process had clear red flags that, when triggered, required review by the executive before override. And most importantly, their metrics didn't just track speed; they tracked trust.

They paused the release. Spent two weeks rewriting backward-compatibility patches. Took a hit on their press cycle. But when the release shipped, it held. Clients didn't churn. No emergency patches were needed. And the trust they preserved, internally and externally, became leverage for future cycles. No one had to lie. No one had to hide. That's what integrity looks like: not the absence of error, but the presence of structure that allows systems to respond with discipline.

This kind of design doesn't happen by accident. It lives in what I call the **Integrity Loop**, a continuous rhythm of four behaviors: *Commitment, Measurement, Correction, and Reflection*. When these steps operate in sync, integrity compounds. When any are missing, drift sets in.

Commitment is where integrity begins. It's not about ambition. It's about clarity. Vague goals create wiggle room. Overcommitted roadmaps invite quiet compromise. Healthy systems treat commitments as design constraints, not aspirational slogans. They ensure that the people doing the work are involved in shaping the promise.

Measurement translates commitment into a signal. But measurement with integrity means more than just tracking. It means choosing metrics that reflect reality, not vanity, not appearance. Systems rot when leaders are more concerned with how a dashboard looks than what it hides. Measurement should expose weakness early, not dress it up.

Correction is the muscle memory of operational integrity. Most systems tolerate too much friction here. People are afraid to raise issues. When they do, the response is punishment or deflection. But in healthy systems, correction is de-risked. It's expected. Feedback loops are fast, and correction is structurally enabled, not reliant on courage or status.

Finally, reflection closes the loop. Without reflection, systems don't learn. They repeat. When teams don't take time to ask what went wrong and what went right, integrity becomes episodic rather than embedded. Reflection isn't just postmortems. It's design evolution. It ensures that what was learned becomes what is built.

In both the Boeing story and the B2B release decision, the stakes were different, but the pattern is the same. In one case, the loop failed. In the other, it held. And the difference wasn't the people. It was the structure.

This is the uncomfortable truth about operational integrity: it's not a function of effort. It's a function of design. More virtuous people do not necessarily run high-integrity systems. They're run by people who don't have to choose between integrity and delivery, because the system makes integrity operationally viable.

If your organization consistently hits targets but does so by bending rules, skipping steps, hiding errors, or redefining success mid-stream, you don't have a high-performing culture. You have a performance illusion. And that illusion is fragile.

So ask the hard questions. Are commitments grounded or theatrical? Do metrics expose or obscure? Have issues surfaced or softened? Is reflection a ritual or a relic?

Because integrity isn't a value you write on the wall. It's a system you reinforce in every decision. And over time, that system builds something far rarer than success.

It builds trust that lasts.

# Chapter 10: Accountability Without Surveillance

In many organizations, the instinct to monitor is deeply ingrained. It stems from a long-standing belief that visibility guarantees control, that if you can see what people are doing, you can ensure that things are getting done. This model worked well in industrial contexts where output was physical, and timing was observable. But modern work doesn't move on conveyor belts. It flows across teams, tools, time zones, and decision layers. Visibility no longer ensures alignment, and control no longer equates to trust.

What operationally excellent systems understand is that accountability isn't created by watching. It's made by designing environments where people can see themselves in the outcome, where the systems themselves support ownership, clarity, and follow-through. But even as we advocate for what I call **transparent autonomy**, it's essential to acknowledge the constraints. Not every role can operate with complete discretion. In compliance-heavy environments, in customer-facing roles, in critical safety contexts, autonomy must be balanced with boundaries. Systems must not only encourage responsibility, but they must also protect against drift, error, and inconsistency.

Too often, organizations oscillate between extremes. When performance slips or outcomes falter, they tend to shift toward surveillance. Tools are introduced to track keystrokes, log status updates, and monitor presence. The thinking is simple: if people are seen, they'll behave. But this visibility creates a different kind of erosion; people begin performing for the system instead of for the work. They build the appearance of accountability instead of the substance of it.

A mid-sized marketing agency offers a cautionary tale. After transitioning to a hybrid model, their leadership noticed project delays and inconsistent client updates. Rather than audit the workflow, they installed a system that logged user activity, keyboard inputs, mouse movement, and app usage. Daily reports scored employee "engagement" based on screen presence. But nothing improved. Morale deteriorated. People felt scrutinized, not supported. Conversations moved off-platform. Real collaboration became fragmented. High performers disengaged, while low performers learned to game the system. Visibility increased. Accountability withered. The root issue wasn't effort; it was a lack of clarity. Project scopes were vague, ownership blurred, and deadlines artificial. The system observed people working, but it failed to explain how the work was accomplished.

Contrast that with a healthcare provider I worked with, operating in a highly regulated environment. Patient safety and compliance required documentation, step adherence, and tight access controls. Full autonomy was never on the table. But instead of defaulting to micromanagement, they redesigned for **operational clarity**. They built workflow systems that embedded checkpoints, automated alerts for missing data, and real-time dashboards tailored to roles. Nurses weren't watched; they were supported. Metrics tracked task completion and escalation timing, not presence. Feedback rituals were baked into shift handovers, where teams reviewed performance openly, identified constraints, and shared adjustments. The result was a culture of ownership within a framework of constraint. No one felt anonymous. But no one felt policed either.

This is the essence of **balancing visibility and autonomy**. Surveillance measures activity. Transparent systems measure outcomes. Surveillance enforces presence. Transparent systems reinforce commitment. The goal isn't less oversight, it's smarter oversight. Designed rituals, clear metrics, and shared feedback loops do more to foster accountability than dashboards full of heatmaps ever will.

But autonomy without structure has its risks. I once advised a product team that prided itself on being "flat and free." No titles, no deadlines, no roadmaps. Everyone worked on what felt most valuable. For a while, creativity thrived. But over time, entropy set in. Dependencies clashed. Priorities splintered. Features shipped half-finished or late. When customers began to churn, blame had nowhere to land, because no one truly owned the outcome. The autonomy was genuine. But the accountability was under-designed. They hadn't built escalation paths. They hadn't codified scope. And without visible systems to track commitments, the team defaulted to assumption and improvisation. Freedom became friction.

The fix wasn't to impose hierarchy. It was to install the structure. They introduced weekly check-ins with clear progress metrics tied to user outcomes. Workstreams were scoped with known dependencies. Decisions were tracked in a lightweight system that made context portable. Autonomy didn't vanish; it got anchored. And as structure increased, trust didn't diminish. It grew.

That's the paradox most leaders struggle to accept: structure isn't the opposite of freedom. It's the precondition for sustainable autonomy. When people know what's expected, where they stand, and how their actions connect to outcomes, they operate with more discretion, not less. They need fewer check-ins, not more. They raise flags earlier, not later. Trust, in that context, is not blind. It's informed.

Building this kind of system requires intention. It requires you to ask not just whether someone is visible, but whether they are *supported in being accountable.* Are there feedback loops that close? Are there metrics that show signal, not noise? Are there rituals where issues can surface safely? Does the system hold shape under stress?

Accountability without surveillance is not ideology. Its design. It's the operational act of creating an environment where people are seen through the lens of impact, not activity, where visibility emerges from shared clarity, not forced exposure.

And when it's built well, accountability becomes cultural. Not because someone is watching. But because everyone is aligned. And that, in any system, compliant or creative, regulated or flexible, is the kind of accountability that lasts.

# Chapter 11: Feedback Systems

Most organizations will say they welcome feedback. Fewer structures for it. Even fewer build the psychological scaffolding required to receive it cleanly and consistently. What begins as an open-door policy or a retro calendar slot often degrades into a cultural performance, where grievances masquerade as insight, where critique is coded through hierarchy, and where the real work of improvement is stifled by fear, ego, or confusion. The absence of structured feedback doesn't just erode morale. It corrodes operational clarity.

To understand this erosion, consider a hypothetical startup with a fast-growing product team. In the early days, retrospectives feel raw but energizing. Founders sit in, designers and engineers debate openly, and postmortems unfold with the messy honesty that builds cohesion. But growth brings complexity. Deadlines accelerate. Headcount doubles. Layers form. At first, leadership continues to attend retros, but increasingly only as observers. Over time, the sessions lose heat. Junior staff members hesitate to speak candidly in front of leads. Complaints about decisions made upstream are softened or buried. On the rare occasion someone speaks bluntly, the air in the room shifts. Side conversations erupt after the meeting. Slack channels light up with private interpretations. Eventually, the sessions become formulaic, celebrating a win, gesturing vaguely at a challenge, and closing with an action item that few will follow up on. Feedback becomes either sanitized to the point of uselessness or weaponized in hallway whispers. People stop saying what they mean. They stop listening to what's said.

Feedback, once the engine of iteration, becomes noise. And the cost isn't just emotional, it's operational. Poor decisions go unchallenged, leading to compounded execution errors. Mediocrity becomes institutionalized, not through policy, but through silence.

The mistake most organizations make is treating feedback as a cultural value rather than an operational system. When feedback is left to personality, mood, or momentary courage, it becomes episodic and unstable. Instead, feedback must be understood as infrastructure, one that's engineered, directional, time-bound, and cadenced. It must flow across multiple axes, top-down, bottom-up, lateral, and at various rhythms, from daily pulse checks to quarterly deep dives. This is the heart of the Feedback Fluidity Grid: a structure that maps feedback along two dimensions, directionality and cadence, and uses that map to inform how and when insight flows across a system.

On the vertical axis lies directionality. Top-down feedback is the most common and least dangerous. It flows through performance reviews, management updates, and executive decrees. However, this axis is incomplete without bottom-up mechanisms, which provide structured ways for frontline workers to surface friction, propose ideas, and flag systemic flaws without fear of reprisal. The third axis, lateral feedback, is the most often neglected, yet it holds the key to peer-driven improvement. Teams that can give and receive feedback laterally, across departments and functions, tend to move with far greater coordination and clarity. The health of an organization can often be diagnosed by how freely and safely lateral feedback moves.

On the horizontal axis is cadence. Some feedback must be real-time, embedded into workflows, rituals, and daily rhythms. Other feedback benefits from delay, a chance to step back, analyze patterns, and reflect more deliberately. A healthy feedback system includes both. Daily standups, weekly check-ins, and quarterly reviews all serve different cognitive and emotional functions. Misaligning feedback cadence, delivering strategic critique in a daily standup, or surface-level observations in a quarterly business review dulls impact and confuses intent.

Nowhere is the deliberate structuring of feedback more operationalized than at Bridgewater Associates, the hedge fund led for decades by Ray Dalio. Bridgewater's culture, often caricatured for its radical transparency, is a masterclass in feedback systems engineering. Every meeting is recorded. Every employee, from intern to executive, is expected to rate others on a series of attributes in real time. These ratings flow into algorithms that map patterns across people and time. But the technology is not the point. The system works because feedback is depersonalized, normalized, and institutionalized. It is not a performance; it is a habit. People know how to give it. More importantly, they know how to receive it.

At Bridgewater, feedback doesn't come at the end of a crisis. It comes in the moment, while the decision is still unfolding, while the learning can still be applied. New hires are onboarded not just into a job function, but into a new way of relating to critique. They're taught not to flinch, to seek the signal inside the sting, and to practice reflection as a shared expectation. While that culture may be too intense or mechanized for many organizations, the lesson remains: feedback, to matter, must be designed as a system, not left to chance.

Contrast this with what happens when feedback is reduced to venting. In organizations that conflate honesty with catharsis, feedback is allowed to fester. A project postmortem often turns into a complaint circle. Power dynamics creep in. The most dominant voices frame the narrative. The most cautious remain silent. Feedback delivered in anger or without context becomes personal rather than systemic. And when the same observations emerge month after month without change, cynicism replaces candor. People stop offering feedback, not because they no longer care, but because they've concluded it has no effect. And once that belief takes hold, the feedback loop collapses entirely. Without feedback, adaptation becomes guesswork. Strategy drifts. Execution ossifies.

But the inverse is also true. When feedback systems are healthy, performance accelerates. A product team that incorporates real-time critique into its design reviews can achieve faster iterations. An operations unit that conducts weekly friction audits learns where its tools fail before those failures scale. A leadership team that routinely invites upward feedback, even anonymized, builds trust by making power accountable to performance.

For feedback to be operationally effective, several things must be true.

First, feedback must be anchored in observation, not assumption. Critique should describe what was seen, not what was felt. Instead of saying, "You don't care about deadlines," a well-trained system encourages language like, "The last three sprints were delivered two days late, which impacted the release schedule." This shift reduces emotional charge and increases cognitive clarity. It also reduces defensiveness, which is the primary blocker to valuable feedback.

Second, feedback must be traceable. Informal feedback systems often collapse under ambiguity: who said what, to whom, and when? Without traceability, accountability fades. That doesn't mean every comment needs a spreadsheet. It means there should be a mechanism, whether a tool, ritual, or role, that tracks feedback over time and enables patterns to emerge.

Third, feedback must be expected, not optional. When critique is treated as a special event, it becomes harder to do well. When it is baked into the cadence of work, into standups, debriefs, and one-on-ones, it loses its charge. Like brushing teeth, the act becomes less about courage and more about hygiene.

And finally, feedback must be safe. Not soft, secure. Safety means the ability to speak truth without triggering retaliation or ridicule. This safety is not created through policy alone. It is made by leaders modeling receptivity, by systems that depersonalize critique, and by a culture that rewards reflection over defensiveness.

The cost of neglecting feedback systems is not simply hurt feelings. It is the slow calcification of insight. It is the loss of adaptive capacity. It is the accumulation of unspoken truths that eventually erupt in exit interviews, Glassdoor reviews, or public scandals. Feedback isn't just a human issue; it's a systems issue.

When organizations commit to feedback as a structural feature of their operations, something remarkable happens. People begin to trust the process more than the personalities. They stop hoarding observations. They offer critique without fear. They listen with the intent to evolve. And they build a culture where performance is not just tracked, it is tuned.

In a world where speed and complexity collide daily, feedback systems are not a luxury. They are the nervous system of operational excellence. When they are strong, the organization feels, reacts, and adapts. When they are weak, they guess, delay, and drift. The choice is not whether to have feedback; it is whether to build for it, systematize it, and use it as a permanent operational advantage.

Let the culture say what it will. The systems always tell the truth. And the organizations that build systems of feedback, clean, structured, and continuous, are the ones still learning when others have stopped listening.

# Chapter 12: Intelligence

In a mid-sized restaurant chain stretching across four provinces, the reviews never stop. Each day, customer feedback pours in, including emails, online forms, Yelp entries, social media tags, and Google reviews. Some are glowing. Others sting. A few offer real insights about delays, food quality, or service inconsistencies. But most are buried in the pile, skimmed, then forgotten. There's no shortage of information. But the loop is broken. No pattern recognition. No routing to specific team leaders. No synthesis of common complaints. In meetings, executives cite that "customers love the atmosphere" and "food quality needs improvement," but these statements are too vague to drive real change. A data analyst once compiled a dashboard with trending issues across locations, but it went stale within a quarter and was quietly archived.

Meanwhile, frontline workers make the same mistakes, managers fix the same problems, and regional directors recycle the same goals. This is the dysfunction of modern data abundance: information everywhere, insight nowhere. It is not ignorance that paralyzes execution, it is signal blindness.

Operational intelligence is not about owning more data. It's about wiring data into the organization's nervous system to change its behavior. Many leaders still carry the legacy mindset that treats data as a passive asset. Something to collect. Something to report on. Something to present in slides. But in high-functioning operations, data behaves more like a live signal, dynamic, directional, and woven into feedback loops that affect daily choices. What matters isn't what you know, it's how fast, how clearly, and how consistently that knowledge moves from collection to action.

This is where the Signal-to-Action Model becomes critical. It describes four interdependent stages: Collect, Interpret, Deploy, and Close the Loop. At first glance, the framework appears simple, but its power lies in how rigorously each stage is operationalized. Weakness at any point, fuzzy collection, flawed interpretation, delayed deployment, or a failure to close the loop breaks the system. And when the system breaks, intelligence doesn't scale. Noise does.

Collection is where most organizations mistakenly believe they are strong. The dashboards are full. The trackers run 24/7. Tools accumulate metrics on customer behavior, employee performance, supply chain delays, marketing attribution, and more. But quantity isn't the signal. Relevance is. An over-instrumented organization can become as blind as an under-instrumented one. When you track everything, you begin to trust nothing. When signals are indiscriminate, decision-makers start ignoring them. They become numb to dashboards and cynical toward insights. This is what happens when collection outpaces interpretation.

Interpretation requires pattern recognition. It involves a separation of event from trend, and anomaly from noise. It is not merely the domain of analysts; it is a shared discipline across every leadership layer. In most organizations, this is the weakest point in the chain. Even when metrics are gathered, their significance is unclear. Are we 10% behind target due to a seasonal lull, a marketing misstep, or a process breakdown? Is customer churn up because of price sensitivity or product friction? Without clean interpretation, data becomes a mirror that distorts rather than clarifies. The result is a paralysis of ambiguity. And in ambiguous environments, urgency tends to override insight. People act quickly, but not wisely.

Target, the American retail giant, offers a real-world counterexample. Their operations team doesn't just collect data; they operationalize it. Through years of developing predictive analytics on purchasing behavior, they learned how to interpret subtle cues, shopping patterns, frequency shifts, and basket combinations to forecast life events. One of the most publicized examples involved predicting pregnancy based on purchasing patterns long before customers disclosed it directly. Ethical concerns aside, the technical and operational sophistication was remarkable. Target was not just observing behavior; they were shaping it. Offers were tailored. Inventory was pre-positioned. Marketing was timed. And all of it moved in a closed, responsive loop. The intelligence system was not a passive observer; it was an active participant in execution.

After interpretation comes deployment, the hardest stage to scale. Data-driven insights often die in committee. A regional operations manager may spot a pattern in store-level theft, but if there's no protocol to act on that pattern, no process for disseminating the insight, no budget to test interventions, no time carved out to operationalize the fix, then intelligence decays. Deployment requires cultural permission to change behavior based on the data. It also requires speed. Many organizations collect data weekly, analyze it monthly, make decisions quarterly, and take action annually. By the time an insight becomes actionable, the signal has shifted, and the response is irrelevant.

The final, and most often ignored stage, is closing the loop. Without it, data becomes episodic. A team may act on an insight, but unless there's a built-in mechanism to review the effect of that action, the system never evolves. Closing the loop means asking: Did the change work? Did the behavior shift? Did the metric move? Was the data right in the first place? It turns intelligence from a one-way flow into a cyclical force. This is where real operational learning happens, not just when decisions are made, but when they are revisited, recalibrated, and re-learned from.

Let's return to the hypothetical restaurant chain. Imagine if their review collection process had an active triage function, flagging any repeated complaints across multiple locations within 72 hours. Imagine if regional managers had structured feedback sessions with location leads that interpreted this data, rooted the issues in process, not people, and experimented with specific changes. Then, imagine those changes being tracked, measured, and reviewed monthly, not just for compliance, but for performance impact. This chain wouldn't just be reactive. It would be intelligent. Not because it collected more reviews, but because it operationalized them.

The contrast is not theoretical. Organizations that rely on data as a storytelling device, something to impress stakeholders, end up with beautiful slides and broken systems. They mistake correlation for causation. They cherry-pick metrics to validate bias. They showcase improvement while execution stagnates. Meanwhile, organizations that treat data as a real-time operating system make decisions faster, correct mistakes earlier, and innovate with far greater confidence.

But there's a subtler difference as well: emotional tone. In low-intelligence organizations, people are overwhelmed by reports but feel blind in the field. They make gut calls and hope for forgiveness. They get ambushed by problems they could have predicted. They defend bad decisions with statements like "we didn't see it coming." These environments foster anxiety, defensiveness, and strategic fatigue. In contrast, high-intelligence environments feel calmer. People are not guessing. They are not overreacting. They are in tune with what's emerging, not just what's been reported. The work becomes more responsive and less reactive. There is trust in the system.

It is important not to romanticize data. Operational intelligence is not about precision for its own sake. It's about usefulness. Many decisions will still rely on judgment, gut, and experience. But when those decisions are made in concert with clear signals, not in defiance of them, execution tightens. Risk decreases. Leverage grows.

The discipline of operational intelligence requires more than dashboards and data teams. It requires leaders who ask sharper questions. It requires rituals that surface weak signals before they grow into crises. It requires technologies that connect dots, not just collect them. And above all, it requires a culture that values not just knowing things, but changing things based on what is known.

Information is not scarce. Actionable clarity is. Intelligence is not the presence of more data, but the absence of uncertainty where it matters most. In the end, the organizations that win will not be the ones that see the most. They'll be the ones that build feedback systems so well, they no longer need to see everything, because the right signals already move, at the right time, to the right hands.

# Chapter 13: Focus and Signal Detection

The CEO sits behind a custom-height desk surrounded by glass walls and four oversized monitors. Slack pings every few seconds. There's a live metrics dashboard on the left, investor emails on the right, team messages coming through on WhatsApp and Signal, and a task list from a virtual chief of staff who thinks in subtasks and recurring check-ins. Everyone wants a piece of the strategy. Every function screams for prioritization. Numbers bounce, people nudge, alerts arrive. There's no silence, only inputs. And what once felt like the thrilling pulse of a growing company now feels like being buried alive under the pretense of being "in the loop." The company is not short on information. It is choking on it.

This is not just a tech startup story. This is the modern condition of leadership. We do not lack data, opinions, updates, or performance snapshots. We cannot filter. We mistake awareness for wisdom. We conflate connection with clarity. And the deeper the organization grows, the more urgent the problem becomes. Because as the stakes rise, distractions multiply. Execution fragments. And unless signal detection becomes an operational discipline, not just a personal skill, the organization drifts into reactive mode without ever noticing the shift.

The human brain wasn't designed to hold competing data streams in real time while maintaining deep, original thought. Nor was any team built to process continuous change without friction. But modern operations behave as if more information equals more control. That's the trap. What matters is not how much you know. It's about identifying and acting on the proper signal at the right time, and ignoring everything else. Focus is not a luxury. In high-stakes execution, focus is on infrastructure.

Operational focus is not just a matter of willpower or personality. It's a designed behavior, scaffolded through systems, norms, and expectations that make clarity possible amid complexity. It is a collective discipline that moves through four distinct stages, described in the Signal Filter Loop: Context, Criteria, Confirmation, and Cut. Without this loop embedded into decision environments, even well-intentioned teams revert to noise-reactivity. They don't know what to ignore. So they treat everything as equal, and momentum dies.

Context is the anchor point. Before you can evaluate any signal, whether it's a customer complaint, a change in market metrics, or a team dispute, you have to know what game you're playing. What's the time horizon? What's the strategic priority in this moment, this quarter, this year? Context allows signals to be judged relative to what matters. Without it, teams overreact to minor anomalies or underreact to major ones. A drop in engagement might mean disaster during a launch, but it might mean nothing during a test cycle. A single VIP client's feedback might demand product adjustment if churn risk is high, but it is irrelevant if the strategy is to widen the base. Context is what keeps the organization aligned to signal relevance. It's the lens, not the content.

Criteria come next. What thresholds make a signal worth acting on? This is where many organizations drift. Without clear criteria, signal processing becomes emotional. A strong opinion from a founder weighs more than a performance metric. A single investor's comment can change the direction of the roadmap. A vague sense of discontent from a team reshuffle of priorities. Criteria anchor signal strength in facts. They define what qualifies as a pattern, what scale matters, what timelines are valid, and what strategic objectives are non-negotiable. If criteria aren't codified, teams argue about symptoms instead of diagnosing systems.

Then comes confirmation. This isn't about over-validating decisions into paralysis, but about checking signal integrity before deploying energy. Has the same issue surfaced across functions? Is the data consistent? Is there corroboration from multiple independent sources? In organizations that move too fast without confirmation, teams fall into false positives. A single misinterpreted data spike changes campaigns. An outlier customer drives product changes that alienate the core base. Leaders lose credibility because their decisions lack a solid foundation. Confirmation is not about delay; it's about velocity with accuracy. It ensures that focus does not become fixation on the wrong thing.

Finally, the most overlooked discipline: Cut. What will you deliberately ignore? What inputs will you stop tracking? What conversations will you opt out of? This is not a passive absence. It is an active decision to narrow attention to preserve bandwidth. Cutting is a way to protect the team's attention span and creative energy. Without it, even a good strategy erodes under the weight of adjacent obligations. This is where operational courage lives, not in saying yes to priorities, but in saying no to distractions that pretend to be urgent.

Let's return to our hypothetical CEO. Now imagine if her dashboard were restructured around Signal Filter Loops. Each quadrant is framed by context: quarterly goals, live thresholds, confirmation sources, and known noise categories. Her communications filtered through a gatekeeping layer, not an assistant, but a triage protocol where only signal-matched items reached her focus layer. Investor updates are parsed weekly against pre-defined evaluation criteria, not read reactively mid-meeting. And Slack? Quiet. Channels reduced, not expanded. Notifications are paused by default. She wouldn't be less informed. She'd be more in control. Not because she knows everything, but because she's finally able to filter what matters most.

Basecamp, the project management company, designed this into its operating system early. They deliberately reduced internal communication channels. There are no constant Slack rooms. They push updates asynchronously. Meetings are rare. People don't ping each other for trivial alignment. And yet, execution continues on time, with clarity, without crisis. Not because Basecamp is slower. Because Basecamp is focused, its system design assumes that distraction is the default. And so the culture pre-emptively defends against it.

Contrast that with startups or scaleups that try to "stay agile" by opening every channel, replying to every thread, reacting to every tweet, and responding to every investor opinion like it's gospel. These organizations burn out not from workload, but from signal fatigue. Employees grow cynical. "We're just chasing noise again," someone mutters after the fifth roadmap pivot. And slowly, without announcement, people stop listening. Not because they don't care, but because no one taught them how to filter.

Signal-rich organizations are not necessarily quieter. But their noise has shape. Information travels with purpose. Criteria for action are known. Teams trust that not every anomaly will hijack their week. There's a psychological safety in a designed focus. People perform better not just because they're working on the right things, but because they're free from the cognitive load of everything else.

In highly stressful environments, even high performers can collapse. The problem isn't capacity, it's friction. Decision meetings get flooded. Priorities multiply. Time disappears into status updates. And slowly, excellence gets replaced with velocity theater, where everyone moves fast, but no one moves forward.

The real tragedy is that many of these organizations believe they are agile. But agility without signal focus is just flailing. True operational agility requires signal discipline. It means training the organization to distinguish between information and direction. Between awareness and decision. Between updates and insight. And that training must be built into culture, not left to individual heroic effort.

Signal detection is no longer a competitive edge; it's an existential requirement. In an era where every function is tracked, every move generates data, and every stakeholder has a voice, leadership must evolve from signal consumers to signal architects. This doesn't mean knowing everything. It means designing systems where the right things rise to the top and the rest are respectfully cut.

You cannot scale excellence without focus. You cannot maintain alignment without signal discipline. And you cannot lead in complexity without learning to hear the signal through the noise. The work begins not with better dashboards or faster updates, but with a sharper filter. One that says: Here's what matters now. And everything else? It can wait.

# Chapter 14: Scaling Execution

There's a fantasy that haunts ambitious operators, a fantasy where growth is assumed to be linear, scalable, and simply a matter of adding bodies, departments, or dollars. The dream goes like this: you take a winning team, replicate it, then expand. A second office here, a regional hub there, maybe a few new verticals, and before long, you've become "multi-market" or "global." But scaling isn't multiplication. It's choreography. And the difference between the two is often the difference between temporary acceleration and sustainable momentum.

Scaling execution is not about the size of your team, your funding round, or even your customer base. It's about how the operational engine behaves under increased load. You don't know if your execution model scales until you ask it to hold more weight, move faster, and operate in more complex terrain, without collapsing. Most companies don't test this gently. They find out the hard way, in the middle of growth spurts that feel like organizational whiplash. Processes buckle. Decision velocity slows—accountability fractures. And leaders discover that the things that made them excellent at one size now work against them at the next.

At the heart of sustainable scale lies a discipline most companies underestimate: the architecture of executional capacity. Not capacity in terms of available resources, but in the precise interplay of clarity, cadence, constraints, and coaching, the core components of what we call the Execution Scaling Matrix. Without these four, scale doesn't enhance performance. It dilutes it.

The first pillar is clarity. At a smaller scale, clarity is often a byproduct of proximity. Everyone is close to the work. The mission is visceral, unspoken norms hold, and knowledge circulates informally. But as teams grow and functions specialize, that ambient clarity evaporates. Suddenly, what was once intuitively known now has to be explicitly communicated. Roles, priorities, and definitions of "done" must be systematized. This transition, though subtle, is brutal. Most teams stumble not because their vision is unclear, but because the clarity that used to live in the room doesn't travel across rooms, let alone continents.

Next comes cadence, the rhythm of operational life. At scale, inconsistent rhythms break systems. Daily standups in one office mean nothing if another team moves on a quarterly pulse. Feedback loops that worked in single-function teams fall apart when cross-functional dependencies grow. If cadence isn't synchronized across layers, the organization starts moving in staccato: surges of frantic effort followed by long silences, handoffs that come too soon or too late, and progress that's difficult to measure because no one's working off the same clock. Without cadence, clarity collapses under time pressure.

Then there are constraints. The myth of scale is that it brings freedom. But in truth, scale demands constraint, not to limit creativity, but to channel it. Constraints protect standards. They prevent teams from reinventing core processes in incompatible ways. They ensure that legal, brand, security, and delivery norms don't fragment under pressure. But most organizations don't build constraints proactively. They add them as reactions, following the breach, lawsuit, and customer churn. Constraints must be deliberate, embedded in architecture from the beginning, not tacked on once damage is done. Otherwise, scale breeds fragmentation.

Finally, the most human pillar: coaching. In the early stages, leadership can model behavior by presence. But scale demands transmission. Execution must not only be explained but taught, internalized, and reinforced by others. Middle managers, team leaders, and regional operators don't just manage people; they carry the executional DNA of the company. And if they haven't been trained in how to replicate the discipline, the system will degrade with each new layer. Coaching isn't mentorship. It's operational stewardship. And it's often the first thing sacrificed in the name of speed, when ironically, it's the very thing that sustains speed over time.

To see what happens when this matrix fails, consider the hypothetical case of an event production company that finds sudden success hosting high-touch conferences. Their core team is tight: production managers who know each other's rhythms, vendors they've worked with for years, SOPs embedded in shared intuition. But success brings expansion. They book events in new cities. They hire regional teams. And they assume the magic will follow the same formula. Except it doesn't.

In New York, the local team overspends on AV. In Austin, the event schedule runs off-sync, and clients complain. In Toronto, the vendor coordination falls apart, and the keynote lights don't work. What's happening isn't incompetence. It's the absence of operational scale. The original team had clarity born of history. The new teams didn't. The original cadence wasn't codified. The new teams guessed. Constraints were assumed, not defined. Coaching wasn't prioritized; instead, we focused on onboarding slides and a few quick calls. And so, what was once world-class becomes average, fast. Not because the company grew too fast, but because the discipline didn't grow with it.

Compare this to Tesla's global Gigafactory strategy, a real-world case of ambition meeting the brutal demands of executional scaling. Tesla didn't just scale production. They tried to scale industrial innovation, automation, supply chain integration, and new territory expansion simultaneously. At Gigafactory Berlin, the company struggled with local labor norms, permitting delays, and alignment with European regulatory requirements. In Shanghai, they moved fast, exceedingly fast, but had to tailor operations to a local context with entirely different expectations and supply ecosystems.

What became evident was that Tesla's clarity about its goals, coupled with the rapid expansion of battery and vehicle production, wasn't always matched by operational clarity about how to replicate excellence across borders. Cadence slipped as teams worked across time zones without synchronized planning. Constraints varied by geography, but the governance model didn't undergo constant adjustments. And coaching became stretched thin as leadership layers ballooned. The result wasn't failure; Tesla still expanded. But the execution carried more friction than it needed to. More cost. More churn. And perhaps more risk.

What we learn from both these cases is that growth is not inherently good. Growth that outpaces executional discipline is dangerous. The tipping point comes not when revenue spikes, but when the volume of coordination exceeds the capacity of the existing system to handle it. When that happens, chaos appears to be progress until it breaks something critical.

The organizations that scale elegantly choreograph execution like a conductor managing tempo, harmony, and constraint. They know that every new layer of growth adds not just output but complexity. So they pre-empt that complexity with operating systems that scale executional clarity, not just structure. They design coaching into the bones of the org. They embed rhythm in the process. And they treat constraints not as bureaucracy but as the rails that keep the train from derailing when the speed increases.

Scaling execution means making the machine not just bigger, but smarter. It means building teams who understand not just what to do, but how to make decisions when clarity thins. It means treating every additional hire not as capacity, but as a new point of risk that must be supported through intentional scaffolding. It means teaching people not to replicate your outcomes, but your reasoning process. And it means never mistaking headcount for leverage.

In a truly scalable execution model, momentum compounds. Teams move with increasing precision. New functions inherit not just goals but working models. Systems flex under pressure without snapping. And as complexity rises, performance doesn't plateau; it accelerates because it was designed to.

That's not accidental. It's architectural. And if your growth isn't behaving that way, it's not that you're scaling too fast. It's that you're scaling without a choreography. Fix that, and the velocity becomes sustainable. Miss it, and what felt like momentum turns into mayhem.

# Chapter 15: Structural Resilience

Resilience is often mistaken for a mindset, an abstract quality of tenacity or grit. But in the operational world, resilience is not just a psychological trait. It is a system property. It is not what you believe; it's what your organization does when pressure arrives. And the pressure always arrives. The only question is how prepared your infrastructure, your people, and your processes are to absorb shock, reorient quickly, and resume critical operations without cascading failure. When systems are brittle, they don't bend; they break. Operational resilience is what turns that inevitability into something survivable. Consider a hypothetical scenario. A mid-tier payment processor has grown fast, attracting thousands of small businesses that rely on its service to process transactions in real time. The tech team is small but talented, and leadership has focused on speed, shipping features, onboarding users, and scaling partnerships. But one morning, traffic spikes. Not from customers, but from a distributed denial-of-service (DDoS) attack that overwhelms their servers. Checkout failures cascade. Merchants panic. Support lines are jammed. The engineering team scrambles, but no incident response protocol exists. There's no clarity on communication channels, no redundancy built into the server architecture, and no role fluidity to allow non-engineers to triage. The company freezes.

Within six hours, the outage made the news. Competitors seize the moment. Customers flee. And by the time systems are restored, it isn't just infrastructure that's been damaged, it's trust.

The failure wasn't the attack. The failure was the absence of preparation. There was no resilience—only optimism.

Contrast this with Mastercard's posture after the SolarWinds breach shook the tech and financial ecosystem. While Mastercard was not a direct victim, the incident triggered a recalibration of its operational resilience strategy. Already known for their layered security, Mastercard began implementing a model of redundancy that treated disruption as a given. Systems were designed not just with backups, but with live failovers. Regional silos were configured to isolate breaches. Cross-functional teams trained for chaos with simulation exercises, building reflexes into roles not usually considered part of incident response. Recovery wasn't just about restoring data; it was about restoring functionality, communication, and confidence in parallel. This is the logic behind what we call Operational Shock Absorbers: redundancy, recovery, and role fluidity. Redundancy ensures there is no single point of failure. Recovery ensures that when failure occurs, the path back is fast, clear, and prioritized. Role fluidity ensures that when standard hierarchies are disrupted, execution doesn't halt; it flexes. Without these shock absorbers, organizations rely on hope. They rely on design.

Redundancy is often misunderstood. It is not duplication for its own sake, but the intentional design of spare capacity. This capacity is what gives systems room to flex—a cloud deployment with multi-region support. A key process is documented and cross-trained across multiple teams. A communication platform that continues working even when the primary network fails. Redundancy isn't waste, it's risk-offsetting. And yet, it's one of the first things to be sacrificed when budgets tighten or growth targets dominate. The organizations that endure are those that understand redundancy is not optional. It is structural oxygen. Recovery is not the absence of damage. It's the ability to climb back, intelligently, quickly, and visibly. Great recovery processes start with pre-defined incident classes, tiered by severity and business impact. They define roles for response, escalation protocols, internal and external communication timelines, and postmortem standards. They practice under pressure, not just on whiteboards. Recovery isn't just how fast you bounce; it's how coherently you coordinate during the bounce.

Then there is role fluidity, the hidden lever of real resilience. In moments of disruption, the org chart should blur. The question isn't "What's your title?" but "What can you do right now to help us stabilize?" Organizations that survive shocks have people who can wear multiple hats. Not because they're heroic, but because they're prepared. That preparation is cultural. It's embedded through training, documentation, and psychological safety. Without role fluidity, teams wait for permission. With it, they act.

Operational resilience is not a luxury reserved for large companies. It's a baseline requirement for any organization that expects to interact with reality, where storms hit, supply chains stall, key people quit, and the unexpected is the only constant. What separates resilient operators from fragile ones isn't perfection. It's preparation. They simulate what will go wrong. They build cushions into fast-moving processes. They design not just for scale, but for shock.

The failure mode isn't always dramatic. Sometimes it's subtle: a vendor delay that snowballs into customer churn because the team didn't have a fallback. Or a product launch that slips because the one person who knew how to deploy the pipeline was on vacation. Resilience lives in the cracks, places where minor disruptions create downstream chaos. These cracks only close when the systems have been stress-tested, not just approved in theory.

When an organization internalizes resilience, the tone shifts. Teams no longer panic; they mobilize. Executives don't issue blame; they activate plans. Customers don't churn; they notice the speed of recovery and deepen trust. Resilience becomes not just a capability, but a brand.

And most critically, resilience is renewable. Every disruption offers data. Every failure is a source of insight. The organizations that refine their systems after being tested are the ones that grow stronger, not weaker. They don't aim for invincibility. They aim for survivability plus learning. That's the long game of operational excellence, not to avoid crisis, but to absorb it without losing coherence. Design resilience early. Fund it as seriously as you fund growth. Because when the storm comes, and it will, resilience won't be your mood. It will be your margin.

# Chapter 16: Sustaining Operational Longevity

Longevity in operations is not about preserving the past. It is about building a structure flexible enough to survive its creators. Far too many organizations mistake continuity for stagnation or believe the antidote to entropy is rigid preservation. But systems that last do not survive by staying the same. They survive by learning, adapting, transferring wisdom, and embedding mechanisms that can absorb leadership turnover, cultural drift, and market shifts without losing coherence.

Imagine an NGO that has become known for effective grassroots programming across rural regions. It began with a small team, passionate founders, and highly involved program managers who personally piloted every initiative. Their impact was tangible. Donations surged. Government agencies took notice. New partnerships were formed. But growth revealed a hidden fragility. No leadership bench. No cross-trained successors. No process repository for onboarding or decision-making protocols. When two senior team members left, one due to burnout, the other lured by a larger international organization, the cracks widened fast. Programs stalled mid-implementation. Field offices waited weeks for guidance that never arrived. Institutional knowledge vanished with a single exit interview. What had once been a nimble, high-impact organization began missing basic deadlines. The board initiated an urgent review, but what they found wasn't surprising. Everything had been built around individuals, not systems. The very passion that had driven early success had also masked the absence of teachable, repeatable, and transferable operations. The mission remained

86

strong, but the machinery to carry it forward had been improvised, not engineered.

Longevity is not just about keeping the lights on; it is about maintaining the capability to perform under changing conditions, with new people, in new contexts. The hidden asset is not institutional memory. It is institutional transferability. This is what the OPS Longevity Loop seeks to codify: Teachability, Transferability, and Tension Management. These three capacities ensure that operational excellence doesn't die quietly when early heroes leave the building.

Teachability is the first line of defense. A system that cannot be taught cannot scale. It remains trapped in the heads of its designers. Operations that are truly teachable are codified, not just in training materials, but in everyday systems. Expectations are made explicit. Rationales are preserved. Exceptions are documented. The more embedded the teaching is in the doing, the less brittle the organization becomes when a team member exits or transitions. Transferability is the bridge to independence. It ensures that responsibilities don't get stuck in single roles or personality bottlenecks. When you can transfer a process from one team to another without a drop in quality, you're building durability. When decision authority can move laterally or downward without organizational seizure, you're reducing centralization risk. Transferability lives in documentation but thrives in culture. It's not just about whether it can be done; it's whether people are trained, trusted, and empowered to do it. A culture of transferability means the organization doesn't flinch when someone takes a vacation, gets promoted, or moves on. It means that when a process is handed off, it doesn't fall apart in translation. People aren't just trained in the what; they understand the why and the how, enabling them to adapt intelligently rather than merely follow instructions. In environments where transferability is normalized, systems outlive roles. Teams rotate without loss of quality. Authority is not a fragile heirloom passed between insiders, but a robust mechanism that moves to where it's needed most. And that mobility of capability, not just people, becomes the infrastructure for sustainable scale.

But the often-overlooked variable in operational longevity is tension management. All long-term systems accumulate internal friction: between departments, between values, between legacy processes and emerging needs. Organizations that sustain themselves manage these tensions without overcorrecting. They know when to let go of sacred cows, when to hold onto core doctrines, and how to host disagreement without destroying cohesion. Tension is not the enemy. Mismanaged tension is. Longevity, in its mature form, isn't about eliminating strain but about metabolizing it. The healthiest long-lived organizations don't chase harmony at all costs; they create structures that can absorb disagreement, dissent, and disruption without collapsing. This requires a deep operational intelligence: knowing which frictions signal decay and which signal growth. It demands leaders who can distinguish between noise and signal, and who can architect forums where tensions can surface early and be worked through constructively. In these organizations, tension becomes a form of feedback. It reveals where alignment has slipped, where roles are blurred, or where outdated norms are resisting necessary evolution. Instead of reacting with panic or avoidance, they respond with inquiry, adjustment, and often, renewal. This is the unspoken core of operational longevity, not perfection, but adaptability under strain. When tension is managed well, it becomes the crucible for the next evolution of excellence, not the reason for its erosion. Consider IBM, not always lionized as an innovator today, but one of the most structurally resilient organizations in modern economic history. Over its lifetime, IBM has redefined itself from a hardware provider to a services company to a cloud and AI integrator. These transitions were not powered by inspiration alone. They were operational events. They involved transferring expertise, retraining massive workforces, absorbing acquisition cultures, and, perhaps most importantly, managing the tensions between old capabilities and new mandates. Each reinvention was an exercise in controlled disruption. Legacy systems weren't discarded overnight, nor were they allowed to calcify. IBM's operational backbone, its processes, internal education infrastructure, and governance mechanisms, enabled it to evolve without imploding. The company's internal culture embraced transition as a recurring responsibility, not an existential threat. Rather than being seduced by the myth of perpetual innovation, IBM focused on becoming masterful at transition: shifting its center of gravity without losing equilibrium. This discipline of managing handoffs, between eras, technologies, and leadership visions, turned reinvention into a skillset, not a gamble. And it is this deliberate, engineered adaptability that has allowed IBM to remain relevant, not because it always leads the market, but because it rarely gets left behind. The contrast to this is glaring in organizations built on heroism, where one or two executives make all the decisions, and where tacit knowledge reigns supreme, where growth is real, but not repeatable.

These firms often shine in their prime, but fracture under the weight of their opacity. Success becomes personality-dependent. Transition becomes trauma. And no matter how well things worked yesterday, the future remains uncertain because it cannot be taught, scaled, or entrusted to new hands. What ultimately sustains operational excellence is not just strength, but inheritability. Can your systems be inherited without collapse? Can they evolve without a founder's blessing? Can they preserve standards while allowing interpretation? That's the test. It's not whether you're still operating in five years. The question is whether your operations still work when you're not watching. And that's where longevity begins to echo legacy. Because the systems we build outlive our direct involvement. Whether they endure in excellence or crumble in confusion is the sum of our design decisions today. The future doesn't reward control. It rewards continuity.

# Chapter 17: Change Management

Change in most organizations doesn't begin with strategy decks. It starts with discomfort. A project misses the mark. A system buckles under pressure. A customer churns after a preventable failure. Sometimes it's subtle, a growing sense that things aren't quite aligned, that momentum feels forced, that people are spending more time explaining work than doing it. Other times it's sharp, an abrupt drop in performance, a public failure, a broken contract. But regardless of the trigger, operational change rarely starts when it's convenient. It begins when the cost of inertia exceeds the discomfort of transformation.

What separates high-functioning organizations from the rest isn't how often they change. It's how deliberately they change, and how structurally they manage that change without burning down trust or clarity in the process. Operational change management, when done well, doesn't feel dramatic. It doesn't arrive with a bang or disappear with the following leadership cycle. It feels steady. Measured. Embedded. Like part of the rhythm, not an exception to it.

But that's rare. Most change initiatives sputter not because people resist change, but because they resist chaos. They resist vagueness. They resist the kind of change that comes without scaffolding, without accountability, without narrative integrity. People don't reject change when it's coherent; they reject it when it's arbitrary, performative, or emotionally dishonest. Which means your ability to drive meaningful operational change depends less on charisma and more on operational maturity: your capacity to clarify why change is needed, how it will unfold, what will be different, and how the system will absorb the new without unraveling the old.

## The Change Containment Framework (CCF)

In mature operational systems, change is executed using a structured method that can be summarized in a five-part loop:

1. Tension Diagnosis – Surface and name the core operational misalignment
2. Clarity Framing – Define the new intended outcome, not just the symptoms
3. Change Containment – Limit the scope to manageable, testable loops
4. Ownership Assignment – Designate explicit responsibility for parts and whole
5. Recovery Mapping – Plan for operational fatigue, re-training, and iteration

This framework works not as a rigid sequence, but as a loop that can be run at different levels of scale, from small process pivots to enterprise-wide overhauls.

Operational change doesn't begin with reorgs or new tools. It starts with tension, the gap between current performance and future potential. That tension needs to be acknowledged, not spun. When leadership pretends that a change is merely a "refinement" or an "upgrade," while teams are already shouldering invisible debt and confusion, the result is dissonance. And dissonance corrodes trust. Real operators name the tension, not in apocalyptic terms, but in precise, grounded language. They surface the friction without dramatizing it. They articulate the stakes without weaponizing them.

This is where the first failure mode shows up: diagnostic misalignment. A leadership team might announce a sweeping new initiative based on market shifts while the ground-level squad is still trying to figure out how to use the last software upgrade. They're not solving the same problem, and the change effort collapses under confusion rather than resistance.

Let's ground this with a hypothetical: imagine a growing software startup, Callwave, expanding from 40 to 120 employees in under 18 months. The product team, now bloated and disconnected, suffers from quality drift and missed deadlines. Leadership senses "team misalignment" and announces a new agile transformation. But they don't begin by mapping what is breaking in the current system. They jump straight to training, assuming the method will fix the culture. Within weeks, friction skyrockets. Sprints stall. The retrospectives turn performative— morale dips. The team isn't resisting agile; they're resisting a change that wasn't aimed at the real problem. This is failure mode two: premature prescription.

The best change agents start not with control, but with clarity. They don't lead with solutions. They begin by ensuring everyone sees the same problem. Because when people don't agree on what's broken, they can't possibly agree on what should be built. Alignment with reality is the precondition for any operational shift. That alignment doesn't emerge from mass emails or all-hands meetings. It appears from structured dialogue, sharp questions, honest retrospectives, and visible willingness to revise the plan if new data comes in.

From there, operational change requires a second, often more challenging discipline: containment. The temptation during change is to overcorrect. To roll out sweeping reforms. To fix everything at once. However, when too many variables shift simultaneously —tools, processes, teams, and expectations —the result is systemic confusion. The organization loses its footing. Existing feedback loops collapse under the weight of transformation. And rather than seeing gains, the team spends its energy stabilizing.

Here's where the CCF's third layer, containment, acts as an internal guardrail. Change is rolled out in testable stages. For example, the customer support team implements a revised escalation workflow across three markets, not globally. Feedback is gathered. Tools are adapted. Only when performance stabilizes is the change scaled up. This is a change done in rhythm with operational cadence, not as a crisis, not as an event, but as a loop.

Consider the real-world case of Toyota's NUMMI plant revival with GM. Initially a dysfunctional factory, NUMMI's transformation became one of the clearest real-life demonstrations of embedded operational change. But Toyota didn't start with a reorg. They began with a cultural and process-level containment: implementing the andon cord (a real-time stop-the-line feedback system) and layering responsibility into small team cells. The change wasn't introduced as dogma but tested at the procedural layer, expanded only when local ownership took root. Success came not from top-down enforcement but from bottom-up absorption. That's how containment scales.

Ownership, of course, is the third rail of operational change. Everyone wants improvement. Few want accountability, especially during change, where ambiguity creates cover. People wait to see which parts of the change will stick. They hedge. They nod in meetings but withhold real buy-in. This is not insubordination, it's self-protection. In organizations with a history of performative change, employees learn to survive by spectating.

Let's be clear: failure mode three is orphaned change. No one owns the whole system, so each department implements fragments, interprets goals differently, and when results plateau, blame spreads horizontally. Accountability dilutes. The lesson here is not just to assign responsibility, but to operationalize ownership: decision rights, success metrics, performance reviews tied to adoption quality, not just output volume.

But even with clarity, containment, and ownership, change will stall if it isn't emotionally metabolized. This is where most operational manuals fall short. They treat change like a linear upgrade: install the new system, train the users, monitor adoption, declare victory. But that model ignores the emotional residue that change creates. Change disrupts identities. It challenges habits. It questions previous decisions. And suppose you don't make space for people to process those shifts. In that case, not just behaviorally, but emotionally, you'll find them executing the new with the energy of the old—passive compliance. Quiet resentment. Subtle sabotage.

The antidote isn't therapy. It's honest leadership. Operational change must be accompanied by a narrative that respects the past while articulating the future. Not saccharine praise. Not empty slogans. But absolute acknowledgment of what's ending and what's beginning.

This narrative doesn't belong in a slide deck. It belongs in conversations, in team meetings, in one-on-ones, in moments of doubt or conflict. And it must match reality. Failure mode four is incongruent storytelling, where the narrative of change promises empowerment, but the day-to-day still reflects top-down control, leading people to disengage. They stop believing the message. Worse, they stop reporting honest feedback. The trust cost of failed change isn't just emotional, it's operational. It breaks the loop between signal and adaptation.

That's why CCF includes a final stage: recovery mapping. Change creates turbulence. No matter how well designed, it slows the system temporarily. New habits must be built. Exceptions surface. Fatigue sets in. Recovery planning means budgeting time and attention for the operational dip. It means retraining not just procedures but reflexes. It means reinforcing until the new feels like muscle memory, not a foreign language. This stage is where long-term gain is either locked in or lost to relapse.

In the best organizations, operational change becomes iterative. It isn't a single heroic effort followed by stasis. It becomes a rhythm. A muscle. The more it's used, the more trust is built. The more systems stay honest. The less fragile the organization becomes, the better it will withstand the next wave of external change.

One final note. Change, especially in operations, often begins without a name. Someone decides to run the meeting differently. A team redesigns a workflow that's become bloated. A leader stops tolerating ambiguity in status updates. These are not grand reforms. But they are seeds. Every operational improvement, whether local or systemic, starts with someone refusing to accept drift. Someone deciding that clarity, rhythm, and integrity matter more than inertia.

So the real question isn't whether your organization needs operational change. It's about being willing to initiate it, not with fanfare, but with design. Not with noise, but with structure. Not as a performance, but as a discipline.

Because operational excellence isn't static, it's iterative. It evolves. And so must you.

# Chapter 18: Process Mapping for Execution

If you want something to work, map it. That sounds simple, even obvious. But in most organizations, operations live in the space between what's documented and what's done. Teams claim to have a process, but when you press, it turns out to exist only in someone's head, or five conflicting versions scattered across folders that no one checks. Execution, in these environments, becomes guesswork disguised as improvisation. What begins as flexibility often devolves into entropy.

Real process mapping is not paperwork. It's operational literacy. It tells you not just what happens, but how, why, and when it breaks. It reveals not only the steps, but the friction. It exposes dependencies, decision points, and failure paths. And perhaps most importantly, it gives you the leverage to improve without guessing. Until you can see the process, you're not improving; it's just trial and error, dressed up in urgency.

The problem isn't that people don't want to map processes. The problem is that most people don't know how to do it in a way that reflects reality. What they create instead is process theatre: sanitized, idealized workflows that look great on paper but collapse the moment you test them against lived experience. These maps serve no one. They hide risk. They mislead leadership. And they create the illusion of control where none exists.

Real operators map with humility, not ego. They assume the current state is messier than anyone admits, and that the value of the map is not in perfection but in precision. A map is useful not because it captures everything, but because it captures what's happening, including the parts people don't like to talk about.

## The Real-World Mapping Framework (RWMF)

A process that can be mapped cleanly can be improved sustainably. The Real-World Mapping Framework includes five embedded principles:

1. Start Where the Pain Is – Map around tension, not theory
2. Map the Path, Not the Org Chart – Follow the work, not the hierarchy
3. Document Real Exceptions – Don't idealize, show detours and failure points
4. Layer Contextual Triggers – Map not just tasks, but decision criteria
5. Test with the Last Mile – The map isn't done until the front lines say it is

This isn't a linear sequence. It's a mapping philosophy that ensures what gets captured reflects what happens, not what should happen.

Let's start with the first principle: map where the tension lives. Process mapping often fails because it begins with abstractions. A team decides to "optimize onboarding," but doesn't ask: where are we losing people? What feedback loops are broken? Where is the trust fraying? They map from the top down, designing around intention rather than breakdown. But tension is diagnostic. It tells you where execution is slipping. If your process map doesn't center around friction points, it's likely to reproduce the very inefficiencies it was meant to address.

A hypothetical: A mid-sized logistics company, FleetFlex, is experiencing chronic delivery delays across its urban distribution network. Leadership initiates a process mapping exercise to "understand bottlenecks." The operations team produces a standard SOP flow showing package intake, routing, dispatch, delivery, and confirmation. On paper, it's clean. Nothing looks broken. But when a field manager is finally asked to walk the process backward from a failed delivery, the actual sequence diverges immediately. Routing rules change based on traffic, third-party partners swap midway, the mobile confirmation app fails under certain weather conditions, and none of this was reflected on the original map. Why? Because the map followed policy, not reality.

This brings us to the second principle: follow the work, not the org chart. Too often, mapping gets routed through hierarchical lenses. The team that "owns" the process draws the map, usually without involving those who perform the tasks. That's how blind spots form. The map describes handoffs that never happen, approvals that are routinely skipped, and dependencies that no longer exist. Instead, effective mapping traces the actual flow of value or information, regardless of which team touches it. If an intern makes the mission-critical spreadsheet work every Friday night, that's part of the process. Ignoring it because it's not "formal" is how systems collapse during transitions.

In the real world, companies like Southwest Airlines, known for their tight turnarounds and high efficiency, have achieved operational superiority not through hierarchy but through "point of value" mapping. They trained team leads to observe where time, resources, or decisions clustered, not where job titles suggested ownership. This is how they discovered that baggage load speed was being determined not by crew availability, but by a single handheld scanner that routinely jammed. The fix wasn't more staff, it was better tech. Without the right mapping lens, that insight would have been buried.

Now the third principle: map the exceptions. The goal of process mapping is not to capture the ideal state; it's to reveal the adaptive state. Where do people work around the system? Where are the quiet fixes, the undocumented steps, the moments of improvisation that keep the whole thing from breaking down? These are not annoyances, they're signals. They show where the system doesn't support the work, and where humans are carrying an invisible load.

Failure mode one shows up here: false formalization. The map pretends the process is consistent, but in reality, it only works because people are compensating. And when those people leave, or the context shifts, the process implodes.

Let's say your sales team uses a CRM that requires eight fields to be filled out before closing a deal. In theory, all eight fields drive reporting accuracy. In practice, reps leave most fields blank and only update them at month-end, if at all. The manager knows this, but leadership doesn't. So when they decide to automate performance reviews using CRM data, they're shocked when the algorithm starts penalizing top performers. The map said "field entry at point of sale." The reality was "bulk updates under pressure." The map wasn't wrong; it was incomplete. And that's worse.

The fourth principle: layer in triggers, not just tasks. A good process map doesn't just say "Step 4: Approve Document." It asks: under what conditions does this get approved? What does the approver look for? What causes them to delay or escalate? These are contextual triggers, the decision points that define quality, risk, or flow. Without them, a map becomes a checklist. It can tell you what happens, but not why it happens. And without a why, you can't redesign anything; you're just coloring boxes.

Trigger mapping is what allows process optimization to preserve operational intent. At NASA, the Mars Rover mission team famously mapped not just engineering procedures but "mission intent triggers", flags for when standard protocol could be overridden due to time-sensitive signal loss or environmental risk. That level of mapping enabled decisions that saved billions in potential loss. Without embedded triggers, teams rely on experience or guesswork. And that doesn't scale.

Finally, the fifth principle: test your map with the last mile. The person who uses the map should be able to read it, recognize it, and say, "Yes, that's exactly how it happens." If they can't, the map isn't finished. It's easy to design elegant diagrams that impress executives. It's harder to create visual flows that pass the field test. But that's the point. Until the people executing the work validate the map, it doesn't matter who else signs off.

This is where the success/failure contrast crystallizes. Success mode: mapping as team engagement. You bring in frontline workers to co-create the flow. They flag inconsistencies. They tell you where the steps collapse. You embed their feedback. Adoption becomes seamless. Improvement starts immediately because the friction was captured honestly. Failure mode:

mapping as a management artifact. A lean consultant drops in, interviews a few people, creates a PowerPoint deck of swimlanes, and leaves. Nothing changes. The map gets archived. Everyone tends to revert to what has worked before.

The value of mapping lies not in the diagram; it lies in the conversations it unlocks. When people share a common understanding of how work is done, they argue less about blame and more about sequence. They stop operating on assumptions. They see where things bottleneck and fix them before they break.

But mapping is not a one-time task. It's a living operational asset. Every time a new system is introduced, a dependency shifts, or a regulation changes, the map must be updated. Otherwise, it decays into irrelevance. Worse, it gives leaders a false sense of control while the actual process drifts silently. This is how good companies go bad, not in catastrophe, but in invisible misalignment.

So how do you embed mapping as an operational discipline? You make it routine. You build map reviews into quarterly process audits. You train team leaders not just to execute, but to document flow. You use the map as a performance diagnostic, a training tool, and a design scaffold. And you normalize the idea that clarity is not static, it's maintained.

Done right, process mapping becomes an act of operational integrity. It says: We are not guessing. We are not pretending. We are not managing from fantasy. We are willing to look at how things work, so we can make them better, faster, and safer.

Because operational excellence isn't about flawless plans, it's about clean maps that reflect real terrain. And the courage to redraw them when the landscape changes.

# Chapter 19: Feedback Loops That Don't Lie

Operational truth doesn't live in reports. It doesn't live in dashboards, KPIs, or quarterly reviews. It lives in the loops. The honest, unbroken, structurally embedded feedback loops that allow a system to see itself clearly while it's still in motion. In high-functioning organizations, feedback is not just information; it's infrastructure. It's what makes adaptation possible without collapse. It's what makes excellence sustainable instead of performative.

But most feedback loops are broken before they begin. Not because people ignore feedback, but because they build systems that distort it. They reward silence. They punish dissent. They interpret metrics through confirmation bias. They filter upward and dilute downward. So what gets called "feedback" becomes either politically sanitized, chronically delayed, or operationally useless.

This chapter is not about surveys or suggestion boxes. It's about the deep design of feedback systems that can survive pressure, scale, and time. Because in operations, the value of a decision isn't just in how it's made, it's in how it's refined. And you can't refine what you don't measure with integrity.

## The Feedback Loop Integrity Framework (FLIF)

This operational model treats feedback as a systemic design problem, not a communication issue. The FLIF consists of five components:

1. Signal Capture – Where raw data or insight first appears
2. Translation Layer – How that signal is framed, filtered, and interpreted
3. Action Link – Whether the insight results in an operational adjustment
4. Loop Closure – Whether the origin of the feedback sees the result
5. Trust Continuity – Whether the process reinforces or erodes belief in future feedback

Each of these is necessary. Miss even one, and your system becomes blind, or worse, dishonest.

Let's begin with signal capture. In theory, this should be easy. Every system produces data. Every frontline interaction produces clues. Every decision has echoes. But in practice, most organizations design workflows that suppress the signal. They optimize for speed or consistency but not for insight. A delivery fails, and the driver marks it as "customer unavailable" because that's the fastest dropdown. But the truth was a faulty lockbox code. The system never learns. The dashboard shows improved on-time performance. Meanwhile, customer churn ticks upward.

That's failure mode one: false compliance. People follow process, not truth, because the system punishes transparency. So the data you collect reflects the bureaucracy, not the reality.

Consider a hypothetical: a large regional hospital, Stonelake Medical, rolls out a new digital charting tool. Nurses are required to enter patient vitals every 30 minutes using dropdowns instead of free text. It standardizes reporting, sure. But it also removes nuance. Subtle but critical signs, such as anxious breathing and unusual restlessness, don't fit the dropdown. So, they go unrecorded. A series of adverse events later reveals that early warning signs were present but never surfaced. The signal existed. The system didn't allow it to speak.

The second component, translation, is where the signal becomes narrative. And this is where most feedback loops go off the rails. Even when a raw signal is captured honestly, it still needs to be interpreted. And this layer is riddled with distortion. Managers reframe uncomfortable truths as isolated incidents. Executives interpret underperformance as a "training issue" rather than a systemic flaw. Teams hear complaints and dismiss them as edge cases.

Incentives shape the translation layer. When a team's status or resourcing depends on the perception of performance, feedback becomes a reputational hazard. So, it's reinterpreted to protect the story. The result? A loop that spins but doesn't learn. Information moves, but insight doesn't.

In contrast, organizations with mature feedback cultures design translation buffers. They create roles and forums where signals can be interpreted in a non-political context. Amazon's "Narrative Memo" culture is one such example. Teams write six-page documents describing challenges, experiments, and outcomes, forcing synthesis and clarity. It's slow, but it creates a friction-resistant signal. The translation is structured, not ad hoc. That's operational intelligence by design.

Now comes the action link. You can capture and translate feedback beautifully, but if nothing changes as a result, the loop is still broken. This is where most customer feedback systems fail. They collect Net Promoter Scores or churn surveys, maybe even analyze them. But they lack a pipeline to connect insights to operational levers. So the team that could fix the broken onboarding flow never sees the feedback. Or they see it but have no authority to act. The input becomes static noise, acknowledged but inert.

Failure mode two: dead-end insight. The organization knows what's wrong. But it can't, or won't, respond.

A real-world example: several years ago, a major airline received repeated feedback that its boarding process created bottlenecks for passengers with disabilities. The issue was known. Complaint records were clear. However, operations teams lacked the mandate to redesign boarding protocols without a complete overhaul of gate procedures. It took a public relations crisis before any action occurred. Feedback existed, but the action link was severed by bureaucratic rigidity.

The fourth component is loop closure, arguably the most neglected. Even when a system captures feedback, translates it well, and acts on it, it often fails to close the loop with the source. The customer who flagged the bug never hears back. The employee who suggested the fix sees the process change but gets no acknowledgment. Over time, people stop providing feedback not because they're cynical, but because it feels like talking into the void.

In high-trust organizations, loop closure is structural. Feedback platforms show progress updates. Internal systems track originators. Project leads explicitly thank signal sources. This isn't about recognition, it's about reinforcing the belief that feedback matters. It's how you keep the loop alive.

And that brings us to the final, and perhaps most difficult, piece: trust continuity. Every feedback interaction either builds or erodes the belief that the system is safe, responsive, and real. A single bad experience, where someone speaks up and is ignored, punished, or ridiculed, can degrade participation for years. People learn. They remember. And when trust degrades, feedback stops flowing. The dashboard might still look active. The pulse surveys still show scores. But the quality of insight has hollowed out.

Trust continuity isn't about culture posters or town hall promises. It's operational. It lives in the micro-decisions: how managers respond to pushback, whether dissent is welcomed in planning meetings, and how teams treat bad news.

Let's shift now to a success case. Bridgecraft, a medium-sized manufacturing firm in the Midwest, faced a persistent problem: defect rates were rising, despite automation upgrades. The root cause was unclear. A traditional audit revealed nothing conclusive. Instead of doubling down on inspections, leadership piloted a feedback loop overhaul using the FLIF model.

First, they embedded signal capture at the line level, encouraging workers to tag issues in real-time via voice input tied to QR-identified workstations. Second, they introduced a "translation council" of supervisors and frontline reps who met weekly to synthesize inputs into actionable themes. Third, every valid theme had a 10-day resolution window, with delegated authority to adjust workflows. Fourth, they implemented a feedback tracker visible to all staff showing which issues were being addressed and which were deferred, with reasons. Finally, they introduced a quarterly "loop integrity" audit where employees could confidentially rate how feedback was handled.

The result? Within 12 weeks, defect rates dropped 18%. More importantly, employee engagement spiked, not because they got everything they wanted, but because the system proved it could listen and act. Trust rebounded. Initiative increased. That's the compounding effect of unbroken loops.

Contrast that with the hypothetical case of SkySpan, a rapidly scaling SaaS company. Leadership touted its "radical candor" culture and held monthly AMA sessions. But when a junior engineer submitted an internal report flagging serious security design flaws, well before launch, he was quietly reassigned. The feature shipped. It failed. And months later, a breach occurred. The engineer left. Others followed. In exit interviews, the message was clear: it wasn't safe to speak the truth.

That's how operational dishonesty metastasizes, not through malicious intent, but through neglected loops. A system that can't metabolize honest feedback becomes fragile. Not immediately, but inevitably.

So, what does it look like to embed real feedback loops into the fabric of operations?

You start by treating feedback as a structural asset, not a favor people offer. You design workflows that capture signal without friction. You ensure translation layers are protected from ego and incentive misalignment. You link insights to execution with defined authority. You build rituals that close the loop with the originator. And you treat every feedback interaction as a deposit or withdrawal from the trust bank.

When these components work together, feedback becomes not just a monitoring tool but an adaptive mechanism. The system starts correcting itself before leadership intervenes. Micro-optimizations surface from the edge. Risk signals emerge early. Team members feel seen, heard, and empowered. The loop becomes the leader.

That's what separates static systems from living ones. Not how perfect their processes are, but how honest their feedback is. Not how polished their dashboards are, but how much the data reflects lived experience. Not how many surveys they run, but how many conversations they're willing to have when the answers hurt.

Because feedback isn't about satisfaction, it's about signal. And the organizations that learn to hear that signal cleanly, especially when it's messy, will out-adapt, outlast, and outperform the ones still chasing clarity in the rearview mirror.

# Chapter 20: Resilience in Crisis

Resilience is not the same as recovery. One responds to failure; the other prevents fragility. In operations, we often confuse the ability to bounce back with the capacity to endure. A team that pulls an all-nighter to fix a broken system is frequently praised for its resilience. But that is not resilience; it is compensation. Real resilience is quieter. It doesn't show up in dramatic moments. It reveals itself in what doesn't break, in what adapts smoothly, in what absorbs shock without losing integrity.

Operational resilience is the engineered capacity to maintain core function under conditions of stress, volatility, or failure. It's not about avoiding disruption; it's about staying functional in the face of it. Systems built for resilience are not just robust, they are self-aware. They detect strain early, degrade gracefully, and recover without requiring heroism. They scale without imploding, adjust without crisis, and operate with enough slack to flex without snapping.

But most organizations are brittle long before they know it. They operate at maximum efficiency, with minimal buffer and zero redundancy, all in the name of optimization. The system looks lean. The metrics look good. And then a supplier goes down. A key employee leaves—a regulation change. And suddenly, the organization, once praised for its precision, grinds to a halt.

## The Resilience Engineering Framework (REF)

Operational resilience is not an attitude. It is a system architecture. The REF consists of five interlocking components:

1. Functional Redundancy – Critical systems have backups or fail-safes
2. Adaptive Capacity – Teams and workflows can pivot without chaos
3. Load Visibility – Real-time awareness of pressure and thresholds
4. Graceful Degradation – Partial failure doesn't trigger total collapse
5. Feedback Loop Integrity – Systems learn and adapt from disruption

This is not a checklist to be "done." These components must be designed into the operational core and maintained continuously.

Let's begin with functional redundancy. Most organizations don't want to talk about it because it sounds inefficient. Why build in backup capacity when resources are scarce? Why train multiple people on a critical task when one person can do it more cost-effectively? The answer is simple: because failure is not hypothetical. It is inevitable. And when a system has no slack, even minor shocks create systemic risk.

Failure mode one is what I call "single-point pride", when a process, person, or system becomes so central that its failure paralyzes everything. A hypothetical scenario: ClarityLearn, a growth-stage edtech company, has a single developer who is familiar with the whole architecture of their learning platform.

He's brilliant, loyal, and fast. But when he's hospitalized unexpectedly, no one can deploy updates. Bugs accumulate. Students can't access modules. The company bleeds revenue and reputation, not due to malice or negligence, but because no one considered building a second path.

Compare that with the approach taken by Netflix. They operate under the assumption that things will break. They intentionally break their systems using a tool called Chaos Monkey, a service that randomly turns off production instances to ensure the system can tolerate unexpected failure. That's not paranoia. That's resilience engineering in practice. They build functional redundancy not as insurance, but as operational hygiene.

Next comes adaptive capacity, the ability to shift workflow, reallocate resources, or change processes without generating chaos. Adaptive systems are not just flexible; they are designed to pivot. They have cross-trained teams, modular processes, and decision frameworks that allow for decentralized judgment.

A real-world case: during the early months of the COVID-19 pandemic, logistics giant Maersk reconfigured port-side operations globally in under six weeks. They had already invested in adaptive modeling software, scenario planning routines, and decentralized training across regions. So when traditional ports stalled, they rerouted efficiently. Teams on the ground weren't waiting for top-down instructions; they had frameworks that empowered adaptation.

The organizations that couldn't adapt? They relied on static plans. They had rigid reporting lines. Every deviation required executive approval. The cost wasn't just lost revenue; it was lost momentum. Adaptive capacity isn't a luxury; it's the price of survival in nonlinear environments.

The third element, load visibility, is the ability to perceive strain before failure. Resilient systems don't guess how close they are to the edge; they know. This requires instrumentation: not just of machines, but of workflows and people. Real-time dashboards. Stress markers. Slack tracking. Task complexity overlays.

Most failures occur not because something breaks suddenly, but because no one notices the cumulative strain. A team runs hot for too long. A vendor keeps missing SLAs. An application scales beyond its design. And when it breaks, leaders act surprised, because they didn't see the load building.

Failure mode two is "invisible pressure." You're flying blind. By the time the warning lights come on, you're already in the crash dive.

Let's consider a hypothetical government agency responsible for disbursing benefits. During a crisis, their application load triples. The system lacks auto-scaling capability, error telemetry, and real-time load dashboards. Staff are flooded. The system collapses. Tens of thousands go unpaid. Later analysis reveals that the system had been operating at 90% CPU for weeks. No one saw it. No alerts were triggered. The failure wasn't sudden; it was ignored.

In contrast, Toyota's andon cord system is built on the philosophy of visible load. Every team member has the authority to pull the cord, stopping production if a defect or overload is observed. It's not just a production safeguard. It's a visibility tool. It builds resilience by making pressure observable and actionable.

Now we arrive at graceful degradation. This is the ability of a system to fail without falling apart. In brittle systems, one failure cascades into others. A delayed delivery triggers a refund, which triggers a billing error, which locks an account. Everything is connected but not buffered. In resilient systems, failure is contained. Alternate flows kick in. Damage is limited. Recovery starts mid-stream, not after the crash.

The classic real-world failure? The 2003 Northeast blackout in the United States and Canada. A single overloaded line in Ohio sagged into a tree, tripping a breaker. Alarms failed. The fault wasn't isolated. Within hours, 55 million people were without power. The entire city infrastructure collapsed, not because one tree was significant, but because the grid had no mechanism to degrade gracefully. The system was interdependent but not resilient.

Success mode: Amazon Web Services. When a region experiences stress, workloads reroute. Services degrade by priority; non-essential processes are suspended while mission-critical flows stay active. Users experience a slower response, not a total outage. The system buys time. It fails intelligently.

Finally, we return to the element that binds them all: feedback loop integrity. As discussed in the previous chapter, resilience depends on a system's ability to learn, not just once, but continuously. Every disruption should result in improved response capacity. But that only happens if post-mortems are honest, if the signal is captured and acted upon, and if loops are closed.

Resilient organizations don't just recover, they recode themselves. They don't just fix what broke. They ask: What made us vulnerable to this in the first place? What assumptions were wrong? What failure patterns are we repeating?

The U.S. Navy's SUBSAFE program offers a striking example. After the loss of the USS Thresher in 1963, due to a series of mechanical and procedural failures, the Navy implemented one of the most rigorous feedback and quality control programs in existence. Since then, not a single SUBSAFE-certified submarine has been lost. That's operational resilience institutionalized. Not through optimism. Through looped learning.

But resilience doesn't build itself. It must be architected and protected. Here's how systems tend to fail:

> They prioritize optimization over slack, mistaking efficiency for robustness

> They reward speed over awareness, mistaking velocity for adaptability

> They centralize control, mistaking authority for intelligence

> They suppress discomfort, mistaking silence for stability

These are not surface flaws. They're philosophical errors. Because resilience isn't a feature, it's a worldview. It says: the world is uncertain. Complexity is real. Failure is not a sign of weakness; it's a design input.

Let's close with one more case, this time, a quietly successful one.

A municipal transit authority in a hurricane-prone region redesigned its entire service model not around normal conditions, but around emergency responsiveness. Every process, from vehicle fueling to driver dispatch, was remapped to include backup paths, manual overrides, and dynamic load thresholds. During a major storm, when most neighboring cities shut down transport, their system stayed active. Not because nothing broke, but because everything broke well. The network re-routed. Communications auto-switched to emergency bands. Teams were trained to adapt, not wait. Passengers moved. Lives were saved.

That's resilience. Not perfection. Not speed. Just execution that endures.

To build a resilient operation is to admit that you won't always get to steer the ship in calm water. That complexity will rise. That risk will arrive uninvited. And that your ability to absorb, adapt, and advance under pressure is not just a strength, it's a necessity.

Operational excellence without resilience is decoration. It looks good until it's tested. But operational excellence with resilience? That's where longevity lives. That's where leadership earns its name.

And that's the kind of system worth building.

# Chapter 21: Legacy and Longevity

Longevity in operations is not the absence of disruption. It is the presence of principles that survives it. Most organizations are built to win today's game. They optimize for current trends, urgent metrics, and quarterly targets. But when the rules change, when the market shifts, when the leadership turns over, those same organizations begin to drift. The tactics that made them relevant become brittle. The culture that once felt tight begins to unravel. Strategy might remain intact, but execution loses its backbone.

Legacy, in operational terms, is not a reputation. It is an infrastructure, something designed to outlive the people who built it. And longevity is not about time served; it is about adaptive coherence over time. To construct an operational legacy is to engineer coherence: systems that retain integrity as the environment evolves, as staff changes, as scale increases. It's not about never changing; it's about not losing the thread.

Operational excellence cannot be considered complete without addressing the question of what remains. What endures after the founding team has stepped back? What principles continue to govern decisions after the original architects are gone? What practices persist, not because they're institutionalized by policy, but because they've proven themselves through consequence?

Too often, we mistake long tenure for legacy. A company that has existed for 30 years but operates in a fog of internal confusion, with no transferable knowledge or strategic lineage, does not have an operational legacy. It has operational inertia.

## The Legacy Continuity Framework (LCF)

The LCF outlines the durable components of operational legacy. It comprises five pillars:
1. Codified Wisdom – Lessons learned are embedded, not just remembered
2. Cross-Generational Competence – Knowledge transfers cleanly across time and teams
3. Strategic Spine – A throughline of purpose and process connects past, present, and future
4. Structural Stewardship – Leaders see themselves as architects of continuity, not just performance
5. Resilience Culture – Organizational identity adapts without disintegration

Let's begin with codified wisdom. This is the infrastructure of insight, the way an organization captures not just what worked, but why it worked. Most organizations are rich in undocumented brilliance. They rely on what one person knows, what a team remembers, and what a retiring executive might mention in a farewell email. But once that person leaves, the operational DNA unravels. Context is lost. Mistakes are repeated. And progress is rebuilt from scratch.

Consider the hypothetical case of NovaBeam, a mid-sized semiconductor manufacturer that built its early advantage on rapid prototyping cycles. Its success was built on one engineer's proprietary calibration process. But as the company grew, no one formally documented her approach. When she retired, her method went with her. Quality control deteriorated. Yields dropped. A postmortem revealed that the knowledge had never left her head.

It wasn't hoarding. It was an oversight. The wisdom had never been made operational.

Now contrast that with Pixar. Every primary film production at Pixar is followed by a "post-mortem" process, an extensive, structured internal review where teams document what went wrong, what went right, and what surprised them. These reviews aren't stored away in a corporate archive. They're used to train future teams. The wisdom becomes part of the system. That's codified legacy: insight turned into structure.

Second is cross-generational competence. Legacy systems endure not because they resist change, but because they make continuity teachable. When a new manager inherits a team or when a next-generation executive steps up, the system must offer scaffolding. This doesn't mean everyone operates identically, but it does mean they operate coherently. They understand the "why" behind the "how."

Failure mode here is painfully familiar: tribal operations. Everything works, but only as long as the tribe remains intact. Processes are optimized around personalities, not principles. Roles are designed around individual quirks. Handover is chaos. The moment a key player leaves, the system doesn't just slow; it collapses.

A real-world counterexample: Toyota's "Toyota Production System" (TPS). At its core, TPS is not a checklist or a management fad; it's a teachable architecture. It's built on principles that guide behavior, not just policies that enforce it. Whether you enter a factory in Kentucky or Nagoya, the operational rhythms, the visual controls, and the problem-solving philosophy are consistent. Not rigid, but coherent. Competence transfers. Identity persists.

The third pillar is the strategic spine. This is the thread that connects tactical decision-making to enduring purpose. Many organizations start with a clear strategic identity, but over time, as leadership rotates and trends shift, that identity blurs. Initiatives become disconnected. Process drifts. Teams lose sight of what truly matters.

Organizations that endure embed their strategic logic into operational decision trees. Every new initiative, every hiring decision, every product line review traces back to core principles. If the strategy was "customer obsession," then even a decade later, operational metrics reflect that priority, not just in slide decks, but in staffing, in incentives, in workflow.

Consider Apple. Long after Steve Jobs' departure, the company retained a core strategic spine: elegance through integration. Their supply chain reflects it. Their product decisions enforce it. Their retail experience reinforces it. That coherence didn't happen by chance. It was architected into operations.

Pillar four is structural stewardship, the idea that leadership is not only responsible for results, but for relay. In legacy-building organizations, leaders aren't measured only by their performance. They're measured by what they leave behind. How ready is the next generation? How transferable is the playbook? How resilient is the structure in their absence?

Failure mode here is what I call "heroic decay." A high-performing leader drives results but does so through charisma, improvisation, and brute-force execution. No one else can replicate it. When they leave, so performs. The system reverts, not because people are incompetent, but because the leadership style was non-transferable.

Now imagine an alternative: a founding COO of a healthcare network spends her last two years not on new expansion, but on systemizing onboarding, mentoring successor candidates, and embedding decision frameworks into software tools. When she leaves, the team accelerates. Not because she was indispensable, but because she built dispensability into the design. That's stewardship.

Finally, resilience culture. A culture is not a legacy unless it can bend without breaking. Cultures that depend on a founder's personality, or that require ideological purity, tend to crack under strain. But cultures that internalize adaptability, where values inform action but don't dictate dogma, persist.

A well-known case of failure: Kodak. Once synonymous with photography, the company had a clear operational culture, until it couldn't absorb digital. The legacy that had sustained it became a rigidity. Culture became concrete. Opportunity passed.

In contrast, IBM reinvented itself multiple times, moving from hardware to software, from services to AI, without losing cultural coherence. Why? Because the culture was built around curiosity, not nostalgia. Around professional rigor, there is no fixed identity. Resilience was embedded.

Legacy isn't nostalgia. It's infrastructure. It's the code beneath the brand, the logic behind the process, the integrity within the culture. And building it requires discipline that often goes unrewarded in the short term. Documenting processes takes time. Coaching successors can feel slower than doing it yourself.

Creating feedback infrastructure feels redundant when everything's working. But legacy lives in those disciplines.

Let's return briefly to NovaBeam. After their quality control collapsed, they made systemic changes. They introduced a "process-as-code" initiative, documenting every critical calibration method, storing annotated video walkthroughs, and training junior engineers using immersive simulations. They redesigned their promotion model to reward transfer of knowledge, not just individual output. Five years later, their calibration team was triple the size, defect rates had dropped 40%, and no process was dependent on a single person. That's operational longevity recovered.

But not every organization gets a second chance. Many vanish not with a crash, but with a fade. Talent leaves. Systems fray. Excellence becomes effortful. Culture becomes reactive. And when the next storm comes, there's nothing left to hold it together.

So, what does it look like to build an operational legacy intentionally?

You treat wisdom as an asset, not a memory.

You design handover, not just hiring.

You encode purpose into operations.

You lead not for applause, but for continuity.

And you build a culture that doesn't need to resist change to remain itself.

Legacy isn't just what people say after you're gone. It's what people can still do because of what you built.

That is the ultimate test of operational excellence: not how fast you scale, not how perfect your metrics, not how celebrated your leaders, but what remains when the spotlight shifts, when the founder retires, when the market evolves.

What endures?

Only what was designed to.

# Chapter 22: Avoiding Short-Term Thinking

Short-term thinking is the silent saboteur of operational excellence. It doesn't scream. It whispers. It rationalizes. It hides behind KPIs and boardroom targets, cloaked in the language of pragmatism and agility. But behind the curtain, it erodes structural integrity, incentivizes shortcuts, and compromises resilience in the name of speed.

You can spot it when teams skip root cause analysis because "we just need to move fast." When new systems are built on brittle code, "just to get something out the door." When process improvements are shelved until "after this quarter's numbers are in." Each choice might make sense in isolation. But stacked together, they build a hollow infrastructure, one that can't bear the weight of long-term execution.

Short-termism isn't just a cultural issue. It's operational rot. And left unchecked, it infects otherwise promising organizations with a form of executional anemia: they keep moving, but with less strength, less coherence, and eventually, less relevance.

## The Long-Horizon Operations Framework (LHOF)

To guard against this, we need more than reminders. We need architecture. The LHOF is built on five components designed to embed long-term thinking into operations structurally:

1. Temporal Cost Accounting – Measure cost not just by dollars or hours, but by long-term degradation or reinforcement

2.  Process Half-Life Audits – Review every critical workflow for durability under change
3.  Durability Incentives – Tie rewards to sustained performance, not temporary metrics
4.  Operational Forecasting – Model systems against multiple future scenarios, not just current loads
5.  Institutional Memory Systems – Capture and reuse insight systematically, not episodically

Let's begin with temporal cost accounting. In most organizations, cost is measured narrowly: financial outlay, time spent, opportunity lost. But long-term operators look at cost through a different lens: How does this decision increase or decrease future optionality? What friction does it introduce later? What rework will it generate down the line?

A hypothetical: Imagine a fast-scaling healthtech company, MediSpan, about to launch a platform upgrade. The engineering team flags that the proposed implementation cuts corners on database indexing. It will save six weeks now, but will likely slow queries by 30% once customer volume increases. Leadership decides to proceed anyway: "We'll fix it in Q2." But Q2 arrives with a bigger launch. The backlog grows. Performance degrades. Eventually, they're forced into a six-month replatforming project, at 10x the original cost.

The original decision wasn't made out of malice. It was driven by short-term bias. And it cost them their velocity, their user satisfaction, and nearly their funding round. If they had used temporal cost accounting, they would have seen the future drag. But the illusion of speed blinded them.

Compare this with Amazon's "two-way door" vs. "one-way door" philosophy. For reversible decisions, they make decisions quickly. However, for irreversible ones, such as those that shape infrastructure, culture, or platform architecture, they slow down. They assess future impact explicitly. That is not just strategic wisdom, it's operational discipline.

Second: process half-life audits. Every operational process has a decay curve. What works today might become a liability tomorrow, not because it was bad, but because conditions changed. Organizations rarely audit process durability. They improve what's broken, but don't stress test what's functional. And so, outdated workflows persist, silently constraining progress.

Failure mode: "legacy friction." You've likely seen it: a new initiative stalls because an old procurement policy doesn't accommodate agile vendor onboarding. Or a customer success team can't scale because their support structure was built for 100 clients, not 10,000.

A real-world success case: Atlassian, makers of Jira and Confluence, embed internal "decay reviews" into their ops rhythm. Every quarter, teams are asked to identify what process, if left untouched, will create the most drag in twelve months. They use these reviews not just to fix, but to forecast friction. It makes a culture where maintaining operational relevance is a proactive, structural behavior, not a reactive scramble.

Third is durability incentives. Too many reward systems are wired for short-term dopamine: salespeople are rewarded for bookings regardless of churn; project managers are promoted for hitting deadlines irrespective of code quality; ops leads are praised for cost-cutting regardless of morale loss.

When rewards reinforce short-term metrics without accountability for long-term consequences, organizations optimize for illusion over integrity. But incentives can be restructured. Imagine if a support manager's bonus depended not on weekly resolution time, but on six-month net retention. Or if a DevOps lead was evaluated not only on uptime, but also on time-to-recover after failure. Suddenly, the incentives shift from speed to sustainability.

One hypothetical scenario: Axion Freight, a logistics firm, redesigned its warehouse bonus program. Instead of incentivizing pick rate alone, they added a long-term accuracy metric, fewer returns, and fewer complaints. Within a year, error rates dropped 40%. Throughput barely dipped. Workers optimized not for output at any cost, but for quality that held over time. The long-term came into view because it was paid attention to.

The fourth element, operational forecasting, is less about prediction and more about stress exposure. It asks: What happens to our workflows if demand triples? If the team halves? If regulation changes? If AI tools are integrated faster than we expect? Most operational models assume today's inputs extend forward. But reality doesn't work that way.

Real-world example: Netflix's legendary "Simian Army" tools. As noted earlier, tools like Chaos Monkey inject failure into live systems. But they also use predictive modeling tools to assess what parts of the infrastructure would fail under unlikely but plausible scenarios: sudden traffic spikes, data center outages, or upstream service failures. By exposing operational fragility before it's tested in public, they harden the system's long-term viability.

Compare this with companies caught flat-footed during COVID-19. Retailers with centralized supply chains had no flexibility. Education platforms built on single-point video providers crumbled under load. They hadn't tested their operational design under alternative futures. And when the world changed, they couldn't adapt fast enough.

Finally, institutional memory systems. The fastest way to repeat mistakes is to forget them. Yet most teams lack structural memory. Lessons are stored in heads or buried in post-mortem folders no one reads. Long-term operational thinkers treat experience like code: it must be documented, versioned, and reused.

Failure mode: déjà vu dysfunction. Every six months, the same fix is proposed. The same mistake is repeated. The same project derails for the same reason. Not because people are foolish, but because memory was never made operational.

Contrast with the approach of the U.S. Navy's Nuclear Power Program. Every incident, however minor, is documented, dissected, and incorporated into training. The system assumes fallibility. It is designed for memory. That's why the nuclear submarine fleet has one of the highest safety records in the world, despite operating in some of the most complex and unforgiving environments on earth.

But perhaps the deeper issue is not structural. It's philosophical.

Short-termism is seductive because it offers clarity. The next quarter is visible. The next metric is trackable. The next deadline is enforceable. Long-term thinking is foggier. It requires belief in a payoff that hasn't arrived yet. It involves commitment to foundations that no one applauds until they're tested.

It also requires courage. To defend the process against urgency. To prioritize architecture over adrenaline. To ask not just, "Will this work?" but "Will this still work in five years?" To slow down long enough to think straight.

This doesn't mean paralyzing analysis. Long-term operations don't move more slowly. They move smarter. They spend less time recovering, rebuilding, and re-explaining. They absorb shocks better. They compound better. They trust themselves more because they've designed with time in mind.

Let's close with one more case. A software company, Apex Ledger, faced a choice: re-architect their billing engine to support future international currencies, or launch with a faster monolithic version that only supported U.S. dollars. Engineering argued for the longer path. Leadership hesitated. Revenue goals loomed.

They chose the long-term path.

Eighteen months later, a major client in Singapore requested a rollout. Integration took one week. Competitors couldn't match it. Apex won the deal, doubled their ARR, and positioned themselves as a global-first platform, because they made a choice that looked slower, but traveled farther.

Operational excellence is not how fast you move today. It's how well today's motion supports tomorrow's movement.

To avoid short-term thinking, you must institutionalize time as a design constraint. Not every decision needs to last forever. But the system should never forget that the future is not optional. It's arriving, fast. And every operational decision you make is either preparing for it or deferring its consequences.

The long game isn't won with slogans. It's won with infrastructure. With systems that hold their shape when urgency presses in. With teams who know that "fast" isn't always better, and that "better" means something you can still be proud of when the spotlight fades.

Operational thinking that outlasts the moment. That's the work. That's the mindset. That's the way forward.

## Conclusion: The Continuum

Operational excellence is often mistaken for a final state, a benchmark to be hit, a certification to be earned, a threshold at which complexity stabilizes, and growth becomes effortless. That notion is comforting but dangerously false. The pursuit of operational excellence is not a linear journey, nor is it a one-time transformation. It is a continuum, a loop of ongoing clarification, adaptation, and system reinforcement. What begins as a strategic ambition must evolve into a lived discipline, practiced daily at every level of the organization. Excellence is not achieved; it is sustained through relentless intentionality.

To understand this continuum, we must return to the foundational triad that this book has explored in depth: clarity, execution, and adaptability. These are not independent pillars. They form a closed operational loop. Clarity shapes execution. Execution exposes new clarity needs. Adaptability ensures the entire loop doesn't fracture under strain. Break any part of that cycle, and you don't just lose efficiency, you lose direction, cohesion, and ultimately, trust.

Clarity, as we've seen throughout these pages, is more than communication. It is strategic filtration. It's the ability to distill the signal from the noise, to define what matters most, and to engineer decision environments where ambiguity does not metastasize. Philosophical clarity, what are we here to do, and how will we know when we've done it?, must be paired with operational clarity: Who owns what? What must happen next? What does done look like? The most elegant strategies are irrelevant if no one knows how to implement them. The best tools become liabilities if no one knows when to use them. Clarity is not an aesthetic value. It is a weapon against drift.

Execution, in turn, is not just doing things right. It is doing the right things with fidelity. Organizations obsessed with speed often confuse motion with progress. But the actual test of operational maturity is repeatability under pressure. Can the system deliver when it's tired, understaffed, under scrutiny, or mid-transition? That's when execution either holds or breaks. We have examined how this depends not on heroism, but on architecture. Strong execution emerges from aligned incentives, clear ownership, codified processes, and engineered feedback loops. Without these, performance will always revert to personality and luck.

Adaptability closes the loop. Markets change. Crises erupt—tools age. Teams evolve. An organization that cannot evolve without imploding is not excellent; it's brittle. Adaptability is not about chasing trends or reacting impulsively. It is about preserving strategic coherence while modifying the operational means. The resilient operator doesn't throw away the playbook. They evolve it intelligently, in real time. That's what we mean when we say operational excellence is a living system.

But there is one final dimension worth naming, a challenge left implicit until now: the courage to institutionalize reflection. Just as feedback fuels individual improvement, operational retrospection fuels enterprise resilience. Organizations that endure are not the ones with the best plans. They are the ones who ask better questions. What did we get wrong? What did we miss? What are we tolerating that we shouldn't be? Where are we succeeding by accident rather than design?

This is where we return to the ultimate framework, the Continuum Loop. Think of it not as a process map, but a cultural rhythm:

1. **Clarify** the priority.
2. **Execute** with fidelity.
3. **Adapt** with discipline.
4. **Reflect** with rigor.
5. **Re-clarify** based on insight.

The loop never ends. The organizations that excel long-term are not those that avoid failure, but those that metabolize it. They treat mistakes as instructional data. They treat reflection as a standing meeting, not a luxury. They build systems that not only perform but also evolve.

So, what's next for you, the operator, the leader, the builder?

You now possess a language. You have frameworks, mental models, cautionary tales, and real-world scaffolding. But the real work begins in application. Select one system. Audit it with precision. Gather your team and run a real operational debrief. Diagnose friction—map clarity. Reinforce what's working. Deconstruct what's not. Document. Teach. Repeat.

Operational excellence is a craft. It is not for the indifferent. It is not for those who believe charisma will outrun entropy. It is for those who see the hidden layers, the signals, the tensions, the systems within systems, and choose to engage them deliberately.

The world will always reward operators who think well. But it will reward even more those who believe with clarity, act with structure, and build with repeatable precision.

Your loop starts now.

The Book On *Operational Excellence*

# Operational Models

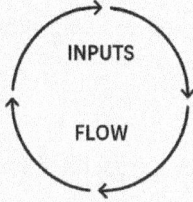

INPUTS

FLOW

SYSTEMIC
LEVERAGE MAP

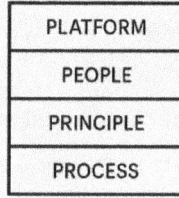

| PLATFORM |
| PEOPLE |
| PRINCIPLE |
| PROCESS |

REPEATABILITY
STACK

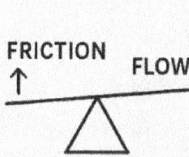

FRICTION FLOW

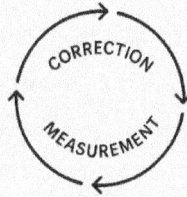

FRICTION
& FLOW

CORRECTION

MEASUREMENT

INTEGRITY
LOOP

The Book On Operational Excellence

Visual Summary of Core Frameworks from "The Book On
"Operational Excellence" — including the Systemic Leverage
Map, Repeatability Stack, and Integrity Loop, designed to help
leaders diagnose, design, and scale high-performance systems.

# Appendix A: Operational Excellence Checklists

These checklists serve as diagnostic tools and action audits across key areas of operational practice. Use them to validate current performance, identify blind spots, and reinforce accountability structures.

**Operational Clarity Checklist:**

> ➢ Have all strategic goals been translated into specific operational outcomes?
>
> ➢ Are those outcomes broken down into actionable, team-level objectives?
>
> ➢ Does each team understand how their work ties directly to the company vision?
>
> ➢ Are roles, responsibilities, and expectations explicitly documented?
>
> ➢ Is there a system for resolving ambiguity immediately when it surfaces?

**Structural Integrity Checklist:**

> ➢ Are operational systems documented, repeatable, and testable under pressure?
>
> ➢ Do systems allow for both scale and flexibility?
>
> ➢ Are single points of failure identified and mitigated?
>
> ➢ Are system owners clearly defined and held accountable?
>
> ➢ Do processes evolve regularly based on new input, tools, or constraints?

**Execution Consistency Checklist:**

> ➤ Are daily, weekly, and monthly execution rhythms defined and respected?

> ➤ Are key metrics tracked consistently and reported transparently?

> ➤ Are there friction points slowing down delivery that can be eliminated?

> ➤ Does the organization default to action in the face of uncertainty?

> ➤ Do systems, not just people, protect progress?

**Decision Discipline Checklist:**

> ➤ Are operational decisions mapped to an explicit framework or rubric?

> ➤ Is it clear who owns what level of decision-making authority?

> ➤ Is the organization able to differentiate reversible from irreversible choices?

> ➤ Are post-decision reviews conducted for key calls?

> ➤ Do decision-makers have access to relevant, real-time information?

**Accountability Audit Checklist:**

> ➤ Do clear consequences, positive or negative, match expectations?

> ➤ Is performance feedback timely, specific, and grounded in measurable criteria?

> ➤ Are underperformance issues addressed quickly and consistently?

➢ Are accountability systems visible and culturally normalized?

➢ Is there alignment between personal responsibility and organizational priorities?

**Resilience Readiness Checklist:**

➢ Are there contingency plans in place for critical operational disruptions?

➢ Have stress tests been conducted on core systems and assumptions?

➢ Is the team trained to adapt to ambiguity without panic or paralysis?

➢ Are feedback loops short enough to detect and correct breakdowns quickly?

➢ Is resilience treated as a design objective, not a last resort?

Use these checklists not as one-time exercises, but as recurring calibrations. Operational excellence is not achieved by intention alone; it's upheld through consistent inspection, refinement, and recommitment.

Build. Audit. Improve. Repeat. That is the rhythm of elite operators.

# Appendix B: Operational Excellence Glossary

**Accountability System:** A defined structure that ensures individuals or teams are responsible for meeting expectations, supported by consequences and feedback loops.

**Architecture (Operational):** The foundational structure of systems, workflows, and processes that support execution and scalability.

**Audit Loop:** A recurring review process used to assess system performance, identify drift, and implement adjustments.

**Cadence:** The established rhythm of operational activity, daily standups, weekly reviews, and monthly reporting, used to maintain alignment and pace.

**Clarity Cascade:** A conceptual model linking vision to daily execution by translating strategy into objectives, objectives into tasks, and tasks into repeatable action.

**Crisis Protocol:** A pre-defined operational playbook used to respond rapidly and decisively under conditions of failure, uncertainty, or stress.

**Decision Stack:** A tiered framework distinguishing between reversible and irreversible decisions to preserve agility while protecting high-stakes calls.

**Drift:** The slow erosion of standards, systems, or execution quality due to ambiguity, neglect, or cultural laxity.

**Execution Discipline:** The organizational habit of delivering on priorities consistently and with precision, regardless of pressure or distraction.

**Feedback Loop:** A mechanism that ensures insights from outcomes are captured, processed, and reintegrated into system design and behavior.

**Framework:** A structured mental model or system template that supports consistent analysis, decision-making, or execution across contexts.

**Friction Point:** Any obstacle, inefficiency, or ambiguity in a process that creates unnecessary drag on execution.

**Integrity (Operational):** The consistent alignment between stated intent and actual behavior in operations, doing what you say, every time.

**Key Metric:** A performance indicator directly tied to operational objectives, tracked routinely for insight and course correction.

**Operator (Elite):** A practitioner committed to clarity, accountability, and sustainable performance; one who elevates execution through personal discipline and system thinking.

**Process Drift:** A phenomenon where defined processes are gradually replaced by improvised or informal actions, often resulting in inconsistency or failure.

**Redundancy:** Built-in duplication or backup within systems to ensure continuity and resilience under stress or failure.

**Refinement:** The continuous improvement of systems, tools, and processes to improve quality, precision, and output.

**Resilience:** The capacity of systems, teams, or organizations to absorb shocks, adapt rapidly, and maintain function during volatility.

**Scalability:** The ability of operational systems to handle increased volume, complexity, or growth without a decline in performance or clarity.

**System Owner:** The individual responsible for the design, maintenance, and improvement of a given operational system.

**Transparency (Operational):** A commitment to open, accessible communication and data flow that reduces silos and builds shared situational awareness.

**Velocity:** The speed at which decisions, tasks, and feedback cycles are executed within a system without compromising precision or quality.

This glossary is intended not as a comprehensive dictionary, but as a field reference. It clarifies language, reinforces intent, and supports the cultural lexicon of organizations pursuing true operational excellence.

# Appendix C: The Operational Models Index

This section summarizes the core models introduced throughout the book, ideal for quick reference or group discussion.

**1. Systemic Leverage Map**

**Focus:** Diagnosing where execution breaks down

- Are decisions and data clean, timely, and aligned?
- Is work sequenced, visible, and frictionless?
- Are issues surfaced early and safely?
- Are problems closed, not just noted?

**2. Repeatability Stack**

**Focus:** Building scalable, reliable systems

- Structured steps for everyday tasks
- Shared heuristics to adapt when the process breaks
- Clear roles and cross-functional trust
- Tools that support, not sabotage, the system

**3. Integrity Loop**

**Focus:** Making commitments that hold

- Grounded, co-created, clearly owned
- Signals that reveal reality, not just performance
- Frictionless issue escalation and resolution
- Embedded cycles of learning and adaptation

**4. Flow Audit (Chapter 5 Tool)**

**Focus:** Identifying operational drag

- Where do delays compound?
- Where is expertise misapplied?
- What systems create confusion or duplication?

# Appendix D: Toolkit Summary: Applying the Work

For teams or leaders who want to implement these ideas:
1. Pick a critical workflow. Map it using the Systemic Leverage Map. What's missing?
2. Identify friction across time, talent, and tools. Treat symptoms systemically, not individually.
3. Use the Integrity Loop as a retrospective frame. Where did execution drift, and why?
4. Ask: Are people executing from process or improvisation? Where is the platform helping, or hindering?
5. Treat feedback as an operational layer, not an HR function. Make response part of system design.

# Appendix E: Recommended Further Reading

## Books on Operational Systems and Excellence

- ➤ The Goal by Eliyahu M. Goldratt – A foundational book on process optimization using the Theory of Constraints, told through a manufacturing lens.
- ➤ Work the System by Sam Carpenter – A practical guide for turning chaos into order through systems thinking and operational structure.
- ➤ High Output Management by Andy Grove – A timeless manual for results-driven managers, focused on metrics, systems, and clarity.
- ➤ Good to Great by Jim Collins – Research-driven insights on what enables some companies to achieve and sustain greatness operationally.
- ➤ Traction by Gino Wickman – Introduces the Entrepreneurial Operating System (EOS), a practical framework for scaling execution.

## Books on Clarity, Thinking, and Decision-Making

- ➤ Thinking in Systems by Donella Meadows – A masterclass in understanding the feedback loops and leverage points in any system.
- ➤ The Fifth Discipline by Peter Senge – Explores the role of systems thinking in building adaptive, resilient organizations.
- ➤ Principles by Ray Dalio – A detailed look into decision principles, culture, and operational precision from a hedge fund titan.

➢ Superforecasting by Philip E. Tetlock and Dan Gardner – How disciplined forecasting and structured decision-making improve operational foresight.
➢ Noise by Daniel Kahneman, Olivier Sibony, and Cass Sunstein – Investigates unwanted variability in decision-making processes and how to reduce it.

## Resources for Ongoing Learning

➢ Offers educational materials and case studies on lean thinking in operations.
➢ Leading insights on innovation, strategy, and operations.
➢ Look for case analyses on execution, systems thinking, and organizational culture.
➢ A curated weekly briefing for operators, founders, and systems thinkers.
➢ Known for tactical playbooks from early-stage startups with operational depth.

These resources are curated not for passive reading but for active implementation. Return to them not as artifacts, but as field manuals. Operational excellence isn't a single playbook; it's a continuously evolving practice shaped by ideas, tools, and disciplined curiosity.

# About the Author

Julian Mercer is a strategist, operational architect, and clarity advocate with over two decades spent guiding organizations from startup ventures to Fortune 500 companies toward operational excellence. Known for precision thinking and methodical execution, Mercer specializes in distilling complexity into clear, actionable frameworks. Through direct experience advising executives, founders, and elite operators globally, Mercer's approach is practical, rigorous, and deeply respectful of the reader's time and intelligence.

Mercer writes specifically for those who demand substance over style, frameworks over fads, and depth over decoration. When not consulting or writing, Mercer is committed to mentoring emerging leaders and teaching frameworks of clear thinking and decisive action.

# About The Publisher

Welcome to The Book On Publishing

At The Book On Publishing, we believe in rewriting the rules of learning. Whether you're chasing your next big idea, building a better life, or simply curious about what should have been taught in school, you've come to the right place.

We're a platform built for dreamers, doers, and lifelong learners, offering bold, practical books and tools that empower you to take charge of your journey. From real-world skills to mindset mastery, we publish the book on what matters.

No fluff. No lectures. Just what you need to know, delivered with clarity, purpose, and a spark of curiosity.

Start exploring. Start growing. Start writing your story.

Read more at https://thebookon.ca.

# Acknowledgment of AI Assistance

Portions of this book were developed with the support of AI. While every word has been carefully reviewed and refined by the author, AI served as a valuable tool for brainstorming, editing, and structuring ideas. Its assistance helped accelerate the creative process and bring clarity to complex topics.

www.ingramcontent.com/pod-product-compliance
Lightning Source LLC
Chambersburg PA
CBHW071700210326
41597CB00017B/2267